THE SCHOOL OF CHARITY

THE SCHOOL
OF CHARITY

Meditations on the Christian Creed

EVELYN UNDERHILL

MOREHOUSE PUBLISHING
Harrisburg, PA / Wilton, CT

©Longman Group UK Limited. This edition of *The School of Charity* first published by Morehouse Publishing in 1991 by arrangement with Longman Group UK Limited.

First published in 1934 by Longmans, Green and Co., LTD

First American edition published by Morehouse Publishing

Editorial Office
78 Danbury Road
Wilton, CT 06897

Corporate Office
P.O. Box 1321
Harrisburg, PA 17105

Library of Congress Cataloging-in-Publication Data
Underhill, Evelyn, 1875-1941,
    The school of charity: meditations on the Christian creed / Evelyn Underhill.—1st American ed.
        p. cm.
    Reprint. Originally published: London: Longmans, Green, 1934
    ISBN 0-8192-1548-1
    1. Nicene Creed—Meditations. 2. Spiritual Life—Anglican authors. I. Title.
    BT999.U5 1991
    238'.142—dc20   90-19825
                                                            CIP

Printed in the United States of America
by BSC LITHO
Harrisburg, PA 17105

To PLESHEY

with my love

CONTENTS

FOREWORD . . . .

PREFACE . . . .

Part I

I. I BELIEVE I

II. ONE GOD, CREATOR . . . 12

III. ONE LORD 24

Part II

IV. INCARNATE 39

V. CRUCIFIED 51

VI. GLORIFIED 63

Part III

VII. SPIRIT 77

VIII. CHURCH 90

IX. THE WORLD TO COME . . . 101

FOREWORD

IT was a great thing for London that we were able to induce one of the best-known writers on the Spiritual Life, to undertake our Lenten book for this year. I have read it carefully through twice, and I shall be surprised if it is not considered one of the deepest and most helpful books of the kind she has written.

The first advice which I should give to the reader of it is that it shall be read through very carefully, first once and then twice, otherwise the deep thought and spiritual experience which underlies it might be missed.

The truths that have gone home most to me (others may find messages in it which more appeal to them) are :

(1) How few and great are the solid facts which underlie all religion. We discuss and dispute over so many things which lie on the surface, but "*I believe in God*" carries us right down into the heart of Eternal Mystery. "The Christian creed," says the author, "is a hand-list of the soul's essential requirements : the iron ration of truths, the knowledge of mighty realities"

(2) The second fact which comes out in this book is *how practical mystics are.* I suppose that Miss Evelyn Underhill is best known as a writer on Mysticism, and yet you could not find a more practical book than this is.

" What theology means by the Incarnation is the eternal Charity of God finding utterance within His creation."

" A Light we can bear to look at, and looking at must adore, comes to us from a Light we cannot bear to look at even whilst we worship it."

" Christ was trained in a carpenter's shop; and we persist in preferring a confectioner's shop. But the energy of rescue, the outpouring of sacrificial love, which the supernatural life demands, is not to be got from a diet of devotional meringues and éclairs."

" The spiritual life does not begin in an arrogant attempt at some peculiar kind of other-worldliness, a rejection of ordinary experience. It begins in the humble recognition that human things can be very holy, full of God."

All these are great sayings and are eminently practical.

(3) That last quotation leads up to another fact very encouraging to us ordinary people, and that is the *capability of all of us to live the spiritual life.*

" After all, the shepherds got there long before the Magi; and even so, the animals were already in position when the shepherds arrived."

" The essence of the story of the Magi is that it is no use to be too clever about life. Only in so far as we find God in it, do we find any meaning in it."

And more than that.

" The child who began by receiving those unexpected pilgrims had a woman of the streets for His most faithful friend, and two thieves for His comrades at the last."

FOREWORD

> " The third-rate little town in the hills, with its limited social contacts and monotonous manual work, reproves us when we begin to fuss about our opportunities and our scope."

(4) But passing over for lack of space the fine chapters on the Cross and the Church—what will stay by me in this book is the description *of the Star-life possible to us here and which will continue in the after life.*

> " We have been shown the sky of stars, enchanting and overwhelming us : and now we realize that we are living the star-life too."

> " We recognize God's ceaseless pressure on and in our spirits, His generous and secret self-giving on which we depend so entirely."

And this life, which is Eternal Life, cannot, it is clear, be ended by Death.

> " I expect the life of the age that is drawing near," and therefore we end in our Creed on a " note of inexhaustible possibility and hope."

> " God is the Lord, through whom we escape death."

> " It is true that we cannot conceive all that it means and all that it costs to stand in that world of purity and wonder from which the saints speak to us . . . but because we believe in One God, the Eternal Perfect . . . so we believe in that world prepared for all who love Him; where He shall be All, in all."

May this noble book stimulate us all to a nobler life !

A. F. LONDON.

PREFACE

IN this little book, which is based upon the principal articles of the Nicene Creed, I have tried to suggest to the modern Christian how close the connection is between the great doctrines of his religion and that " inner life " which is too often regarded as a more spiritual alternative to orthodoxy : how rich and splendid is the Christian account of reality, and how much food it has to offer to the contemplative soul. We sometimes forget that, with hardly an exception, the greatest masters of the spiritual life speak to us from within the Church ; accept its teachings, and are supported by its practices. They tell us, because of their own vivid sense of God, what full life within that Church really means and can be ; they do not invite us to contract out of it. Their chief gift to us, their average brothers and sisters, does not consist in the production of striking spiritual novelties, but rather in the penetrating light which they cast on the familiar truths of religion ; showing us that these truths are many-levelled, and will only yield up their unspeakable richness and beauty to those who take the trouble to dig below the surface, and seek for the Treasure which is still hidden in the field. If these chapters encourage others to explore their resources, and do a little quiet home digging for themselves—instead of relying upon foreign imports, doubtfully labelled " Higher Wisdom," " Eastern Mysticism," and the rest—their main purpose will have been achieved.

PREFACE

The first part of the book deals with the ruling fact of religion, the Reality and Nature of God ; the second with the way that Reality and Nature are revealed within human life, and we lay hold of them ; the third, with the kind of life they demand from us, and make possible. These are truths common to all Christians, whatever their " theological colour " may be ; and moreover they are the truths which lie at the root of all valid Christian action, and give its special colour to the Christian outlook on the world. So, if it be thought that these meditations dwell too exclusively on the inner life and have no obvious practical bearing on the social and moral problems which beset us, let us remember that such a retreat to the spiritual is the best of all preparations for dealing rightly with the actual. For our real hope of solving these problems abides in bringing them into relation with the eternal truth of God ; placing them within the radiance of Charity.

E.U.

Feast of St. Mary Magdalen,
  1933.

PART I

CHAPTER I

I BELIEVE

God is love, and he that abideth in love abideth in God and God abideth in him . . . we love because he first loved.—St. John.

We shall never learn to know ourselves except by endeavouring to know God, for beholding His greatness, we realize our littleness. His purity shows our foulness, and by meditating on His humility we find how very far we are from being humble.—St. Teresa.

EVERYONE who is engaged on a great undertaking, depending on many factors for its success, knows how important it is to have a periodical stocktaking. Whether we are responsible for a business, an institution, a voyage, or an exploration—even for the well-being of a household —it is sometimes essential to call a halt ; examine our stores and our equipment, be sure that all necessaries are there and in good order, and that we understand the way in which they should be used. It is no good to have tins without tin openers, bottles of which the contents have evaporated, labels written in an unknown language, or mysterious packages of which we do not know the use. Now the living-out of the spiritual life, the inner life of the Christian—the secret correspondence of his soul with God—is from one point of view a great business. It was well called " the business of all businesses " by St. Bernard; for it is no mere addition to Christianity, but its very essence, the source of its vitality and power. From another point of view it is a great journey ; a bit-by-bit progress, over roads that are often difficult and in weather that is sometimes pretty bad, from " this world to that which is to come." Whichever way we look at it, an intelligent and respectful attitude to our equipment—seeing that it is all there, accessible and in good condition, and making sure that we know the real use of each item—is essential to success. It is only too easy to be deluded by the modern craving for pace and immediate results, and press on without pausing to examine the quality and character of our supplies, or being sure that we know where we are going and possess the necessary maps. But this means all the disabling miseries of the unmarked route and unbalanced diet ; and at last, perhaps, complete loss of bearings and consequent starvation of the soul.

Karl Barth has told us, that on becoming a Calvinist minister, he paused to examine his own spiritual stock in trade ; and found to his horror that it was useless to him. He seemed to have nothing to feed on, nothing to depend on, nothing to give. It looked imposing ; but much of the food was stale and unnourishing, some of the tins seemed empty, and some were so tightly sealed that he could not reach their contents. He was the child and servant of that Infinite God, whose every word nourishes the souls of men. But he was receiving nothing from Him: the real contents of the stores that had been issued to him were inaccessible. In apparent plenty, he was spiritually starved. In lesser ways that dreadful situation can easily become our own, if we merely take our religious equipment for granted ; do not make sure that it contains food on which we can feed, tins we can open, and that we know what the labels really mean. For the spiritual life of man cannot be maintained on a diet of suggestive phrases and ideas. Only when we have found within the familiar externals of our religion, those vivid realities which these externals enclose and keep safe, are we using our equipment properly and getting the food we need. We must open the tins, if we are to discover inside them the mysterious nourishment of the soul. Nor have we any right to ask for fresh enlightenment, or a new issue of provisions, until we have fully explored the resources we already possess.

This process is equally necessary for those who are repelled by the externals of religion, and those who are attracted by them. Both need to recognize the difference between the container and the content. Many people spend the whole of their devotional lives sitting by the wayside admiring the pictures on the tins; more are alienated from religion by mistaking this procedure for faith. Karl Barth went away into solitude to open some of his least promising packages; and found with amazement within them the inexhaustible nourishment of eternal life.

Lent is a good moment for such spiritual stocktaking; a pause, a retreat from life's busy surface to its solemn deeps. There we can consider our possessions; and discriminate between the necessary stores which have been issued to us, and must be treasured and kept in good order, and the odds and ends which we have accumulated for ourselves. Most of us are inclined to pay considerable attention to the spiritual odds and ends : the air-cushions, tabloids, and vacuum flasks, and various labour-saving devices which we call by such attractive names as our own peace, our own approach, our own experience, and so forth. But we leave the superb and massive standard equipment which is issued to each baptized Christian to look after itself. There are few who cannot benefit by a bit by bit examination of that equipment, a humble return to first principles ; for there we find the map and road-book of that spiritual world which is our true environment, all the needed information about the laws which control it, and all essentials for feeding that inner life of which we talk so much and understand so very little.

The Christian creed is a hand-list of the soul's essential requirements : the iron ration of truths, the knowledge of mighty realities, which rightly used is sufficient to feed and safeguard our supernatural life throughout its course. When Christians say the Creed, they say in effect, " This is what we believe to be the truth about existence ; about God and the things of God, and so by implication about our own mysterious lives." For the whole of life, visible and invisible, is governed by these statements ; which come to us from beyond our normal radius, entering the human scene in their penetrating truth and majestic beauty, to show us how to live.

The longer we go on with life, the more mysterious, the more baffling it seems to most of us : and the more deeply we feel the need of being taught how to live. We go muddling on, secretly conscious that we are making a mess of it. Guides come forward to tell us this or that, yet always with an avoidance of the full mystery of our situation, seldom with any real sense of the richness of the material of life : and they all fail to be of much use to us when we come to the bad bits. The surface-indications often mislead us. The tangle of new roads, bordered by important-looking factories and unhappy little trees, the arterial highways leading nowhere, the conflicting demands and directions which reach us from every side, only make our confusions worse. And at last we realize that only the Author of human life can teach us how to live human life, because He alone sees it in its eternal significance : and He does this by a disclosure that at first may seem strange and puzzling, but grows in beauty and meaning as we gaze at it, and which feeds, enlightens and supports us when we dare to take up the life that it reveals.

" Lord," said St. Thomas Aquinas, " set my life in order ; making me to know what I ought to do and do it in the way that I should." The civilized world seems now to have reached the point at which only this prayer can save it ; and the answer is already given us in the Christian creed. We talk much of reconstruction ; but no one has yet dared to take the Christian's profound beliefs about Reality as the basis of a reconditioned world. We treat them as dwellers in the plain treat the mountains. We lift up our eyes to their solemn beauty with respect ; but refuse to acknowledge that plain and mountain are part of the same world. Yet the Creed is no mere academic document, no mere list of " dogmas." It is an account of that which *is ;* and every word it contains has a meaning at once universal, practical, and spiritual within the particular experience of each soul. It irradiates and harmonizes every level of our life, not one alone. All great spiritual literature does this to some extent ; but the Creed, the condensed hand-list of those deep truths from which spiritual literature is built up, does it supremely.

Dante warned the readers of the *Divine Comedy* that everything in it had a fourfold meaning, and would never be understood by those who were satisfied by the surface-sense alone. This, which is indeed true of the *Comedy*, is far more true of the great statements of the Christian religion. They are true at every level ; but only disclose their full splendour and attraction when we dare to reach out, beyond their surface beauty and their moral teaching, to God, their meaning and their end, and let their fourfold wisdom and tremendous demands penetrate and light up the deepest level of our souls.

The spiritual life is a stern choice. It is not a consoling retreat from the difficulties of existence ; but an invitation to enter fully into that difficult existence, and there apply the Charity of God and bear the cost. Till we accept this truth, religion is full of puzzles for us, and its practices often unmeaning : for we do not know what it is all about. So there are few things more bracing and enlightening than a deliberate resort to these superb statements about God, the world and the soul ; testing by them our attitude to those realities, and the quality and vigour of our interior life with God. For every one of them has a direct bearing on that interior life. *Lex credendi, lex orandi.* Our prayer and belief should fit like hand and glove ; they are the inside and outside of one single correspondence with God. Since the life of prayer consists in an ever-deepening communion with a Reality beyond ourselves, which is truly there, and touches, calls, attracts us, what we believe about that Reality will rule our relation to it. We do not approach a friend and a machine in the same way. We make the first and greatest of our mistakes in religion when we begin with ourselves, our petty feelings and needs, ideas and capacities. The Creed sweeps us up past all this to GOD, the objective Fact, and His mysterious self-giving to us. It sets first Eternity and then History before us, as the things that truly matter in religion ; and shows us a humble and adoring delight in God as the first duty of the believing soul. So there can hardly be a better inward discipline than the deliberate testing of our vague, dilute, self-occupied spirituality by this superb vision of Reality.

These great objective truths are not very fashionable

among modern Christians; yet how greatly we need them, if we are to escape pettiness, individualism and emotional bias. For that mysterious inner life which glows at the heart of Christianity, which we recognize with delight whenever we meet it, and which is the source of Christian power in the world, is fed through two channels. Along one channel a certain limited knowledge of God and the things of God enters the mind; and asks of us that honest and humble thought about the mysteries of faith which is the raw material of meditation. Along the other channel God Himself comes secretly to the heart, and wakes up that desire and that sense of need which are the cause of prayer. The awestruck vision of faith and the confident movement of love are both needed, if the life of devotion is to be rich, brave and humble; equally removed from mere feeling and mere thought. Christian prayer to God must harmonize with Christian belief about God: and quickly loses humility and sanity if it gets away from that great law. We pray first because we believe something; perhaps at that stage a very crude or vague something. And with the deepening of prayer, its patient cultivation, there comes—perhaps slowly, perhaps suddenly—the enrichment and enlargement of belief, as we enter into a first-hand communion with the Reality who is the object of our faith.

For God, not man, is the first term of religion: and our first step in religion is the acknowledgment that HE Is. All else is the unfolding of those truths about His life and our life, which this fact of facts involves. I believe in One God. We begin there; not with our own needs, desires, feelings, or obligations. Were all these abolished, His independent splendour would remain, as the Truth which gives its meaning to the world. So we begin by stating with humble delight our belief and trust in the most concrete, most rich of all realities—God. Yet even the power to do this reflects back again to Him, and witnesses to His self-giving to the soul. For Christianity is not a pious reverie, a moral system or a fantasy life ; it is a revelation, adapted to our capacity, of the Realities which control life. Those Realities must largely remain unknown to us ; limited little creatures that we are. God, as Brother Giles said, is a great mountain of corn from which man, like a sparrow, takes a grain of wheat : yet even that grain of wheat, which is as much as we can carry away, contains all the essentials of our life. We are to carry it carefully and eat it gratefully : remembering with awe the majesty of the mountain from which it comes.

The first thing this vast sense of God does for us, is to deliver us from the imbecilities of religious self-love and self-assurance ; and sink our little souls in the great life of the race, in and upon which this One God in His mysterious independence is always working, whether we notice it or not. When that sense of His unique reality gets dim and stodgy, we must go back and begin there once more ; saying with the Psalmist, " All my fresh springs are in thee." Man, said Christ, is nourished by every word that proceeds out of the mouth of God. Not the words we expect, or persuade ourselves that we have heard ; but those unexpected words He really utters, sometimes by the mouths of the most unsuitable people, sometimes through apparently unspiritual events, sometimes secretly within the soul. Therefore seeking God, and listening to God, is an important part of the business of human life : and this is the essence of prayer. We do something immense, almost unbelievable, when we enter that world of prayer, for then we deliberately move out towards that transcendent Being whom Christianity declares to be the one Reality : a Reality revealed to us in three ways as a Creative Love, a Rescuing Love, and an Indwelling, all-pervading Love, and in each of those three ways claiming and responding to our absolute trust. Prayer is the give-and take between the little souls of men and that three-fold Reality.

So we begin the overhaul of our spiritual equipment not by thinking about our own needs and shortcomings, but by looking up and out at this One Reality, this Unchanging God, and so gaining a standard of comparison, a "control." That remarkable naturalist and philosopher, Dr. Beebe, whose patient study of living things seems to have brought him so near to the sources of life, says in his latest book *Nonsuch*, " As a panacea for a host of human ills, worries and fears, I should like to advocate a law that every toothbrush should have a small telescope in its handle, and the two used equally." As far as the life of religion is concerned, if we always used the telescope before we used the toothbrush—looked first at the sky of stars, the great ranges of the beauty and majesty of God, and only then at our own small souls and their condition, needs, and sins—the essential work of the toothbrush would be much better done ; and without that self-conscious conviction of its overwhelming importance, and the special peculiarities and requirements of our own set of teeth, which the angels must surely find amusing. " Where I left myself I found God ; where I found myself, I lost God," says Meister Eckhart. Our eyes are not in focus for His Reality, until they are out of focus for our own petty concerns.

What then is the nature of that Eternal God, the Substance of all that is, so far as we are able to apprehend Him ?

What is the quality of that mysterious starlight the telescope helps us to discern ? We are Christians ; and so we accept, in spite of all appearances to the contrary, the Christian account of His character. God is Love, or rather Charity ; generous, out-flowing, self-giving love, *Agape*. When all the qualities which human thought attributes to Reality are set aside, this remains. Charity is the colour of the Divine personality, the spectrum of Holiness. We believe that the tendency to give, to share, to cherish, is the mainspring of the universe, ultimate cause of all that is, and reveals the Nature of God : and therefore that when we are most generous we are most living and most real. " Who dwelleth in Charity dwelleth in God, and God in him " ; our true life develops within a spiritual world which lives and glows in virtue of His Eternal Charity. To enter the Divine order then, achieve the full life for which we are made, means entering an existence which only has meaning as the channel and expression of an infinite, self-spending love. This is not piety. It is not altruism. It is the clue to our human situation.

The Creed, our list of the spiritual truths to which our inner life must be conformed, is all about a God who *is* Charity, a Charity that *is* God. It tells us that what we call creation is the never-ceasing action of a self-spending personal love ; and all the experiences and acts of religion are simply our small experience of, and response to, the pressure and the call of that same creative Love which rules the stars. " Behold, Lord, from whence such love proceedeth ! " exclaims Thomas à Kempis. It proceeds from the very heart of the universe. For Christians this is the ultimate fact, which must govern the whole conduct of life. We are each created, sought, possessed and maintained by a living Reality that is Charity ; truly known by us in and through His free, generous self-giving, and in no other way. The life which we are called upon to manifest in space and time is a living spark of this generous Love. That means that the true demand of religion will never be a demand for correct behaviour or correct belief; but for generosity, as the controlling factor in every relation between man and God and man and man. To look at ourselves and our lives after looking at this great truth is surely enough to bring self-satisfied piety down with a run.

When we look out towards this Love that moves the stars and stirs in the child's heart, and claims our total allegiance and remember that this alone is Reality and we are only real so far as we conform to its demands, we see our human situation from a fresh angle; and perceive that it is both more humble and dependent, and more splendid, than we had dreamed. We are surrounded and penetrated by great spiritual forces, of which we hardly know anything. Yet the outward events of our life cannot be understood, except in their relation to that unseen and intensely living world, the Infinite Charity which penetrates and supports us, the God whom we resist and yet for whom we thirst; who is ever at work, transforming the self-centred desire of the natural creature into the wide-spreading, outpouring love of the citizen of Heaven.

CHAPTER II

ONE GOD, CREATOR

The Divine action bathes the whole universe. It penetrates all creatures, it hovers above them. Wherever they are, it is. It goes before them, it is with them, it follows them. They need but let themselves be borne upon its waves.—De Caussade.

THE governing thought of the Creed is truly the first and last word of religion. It covers our whole response to reality. " I believe in One God "—not " I want," or " I feel," but " He Is "—all the rest flows from that, or is a special exhibition of it. Christian history is not the story of a number of individual religious experiences and developments. It describes the self-revelation and self-giving of that one infinitely generous God in whom, because of that revelation and self-giving, the soul believes. All the various forms of prayer and contemplation, or the disciplines of the spiritual life, only matter because they help, deepen, and purify our humble communion with this One God, infinite in His richness, delicacy and power ; who is touching, calling and changing His creatures in countless ways, by the unceasing action of creative love. He is there first, over-passing in His Perfection all our partial discoveries. That which we really know about God, is not what we have been clever enough to find out, but what the Divine Charity has secretly revealed.

And so we go on to make our first statement about this One God who is the controlling reality of life, and try to see what this should mean for our prayer ; that is, our small effort to correspond with Him. Christianity says that this One God is best defined as " Father Almighty, Maker of heaven and earth, and of all things, visible and invisible." No limits are placed to the Divine fatherhood. The universe in its wholeness, and with all its disconcerting contrasts—the world of beauty, the world of science, the world of love, and those mysterious deeps of being of which the spirit can sometimes in prayer discern the fringe—these, visible and invisible, the very heavenly and the very earthy, are the creations of the Divine Charity ; the living, acting, overflowing generosity of God.

In practice, of course, no one can grasp this mighty declaration : nor indeed should we expect to be able to grasp it. If the Reality of God were small enough to be grasped, it would not be great enough to be adored ; and so our holiest privilege would go. " I count not myself to have grasped ; but as one that has been grasped, I press on," says St. Paul. But if all real knowledge here is a humbly delighted knowledge of our own ignorance—if, as the dying artist said, " The word we shall use most when we get to heaven will be ' Oh ! ' "—still we can realize something of what it means, to consider our world from this point of view. It means that everything we are given to deal with—including ourselves and our psychological material, however intractable—is the result of the creative action of a personal Love, who despises nothing that He has made. We, then, cannot take the risk of despising anything ; and any temptation to do so must be attributed to our ignorance, stupidity or self-love, and recognized as something which distorts our vision of Reality.

" He shewed me a little thing " says Julian of Norwich, " the quantity of a hazel nut in the palm of my hand ; and it was as round as a ball. I looked thereupon with the eye of my under-standing and thought: *What may this be ?* And it was answered generally thus : *It is all that is made.* . . . In this Little Thing I saw three properties. The first is that God made it, the second is that God loveth it, the third, that God keepeth it."

That is a saint's comment on the first article of her Creed. It is a vision that takes much living-out in a world in which injustice and greed are everywhere manifest ; full too of tendencies which we are able to recognize as evil, and of misery and failure which seem the direct result of corporate stupidity and self-love, offering us ceaseless opportunities for the expression of disapproval and disgust, and often tempting to despair. " All-thing hath the Being by the Love of God," says Julian again. And then we think of a natural order shot through with suffering, marred at every point by imperfection, maintained by mutual destruction ; a natural order which includes large populations of vermin, and the flora and fauna of infectious disease. It is easy to be both sentimental and theological over the more charming and agreeable aspects of Nature. It is very difficult to see its essential holiness beneath dis-concerting and hostile appearances with an equable and purified sight ; with something of the large, disinterested Charity of God.

To stand alongside the generous Creative Love, maker of all things visible and invisible (including those we do not like) and see them with the eyes of the Artist-Lover is the secret of sanctity. St. Francis did this with a singular perfection ; but we know the price that he paid. So too that rapt and patient lover of all life, Charles Darwin, with his great, self-forgetful interest in the humblest and tiniest forms of life—not because they were useful to him, but

for their own sakes—fulfilled one part of our Christian
duty far better than many Christians do. It is a part of
the life of prayer, which is our small attempt to live the
life of Charity, to consider the whole creation with a deep
and selfless reverence ; enter into its wonder, and find in
it the mysterious intimations of the Father of Life, maker
of all things, Creative Love.

This loving reverence for life is not to stop short even
at the microbe and the worm. It must be extended to ourselves, and the qualities, tendencies and powers which God
has implanted or brought forth in us. We have to discriminate between our natural passions, which are a true
part of His creative material, and the way we handle them,
which is left to us. It is no proof of spirituality to discredit
the fiery energies which He has implanted in the natural
order, and in which we all share. All genuine re-ordering
of character must be based on an adoring faith in the maker
of our wonderful psycho-physical machine, and humble
acceptance of its capacities and limitations. If it is not
running right, the fault is not with the original design ;
but with our oiling and timing and ill-conceived adjust-
ments, our poor attempts to keep it clean and give it the
right mixture, and our pessimistic feeling that it is hard
lines to have inherited the family tourer, with all its
unfortunate peculiarities, whilst others seem to be making
the journey in a well-sprung six-cylinder saloon.

If we do not acquire this habit of looking at the complex
natural world, including our natural selves, with eyes
cleansed by prayer and brought into focus by humility—
if we attempt to judge it from our own point of view, without a loving movement of the mind towards the Creator
of all this splendour, this intricate web of life—then how
easy it is to get lost in it, and lose all sense of its myster-

c

ious beauty ; because we mistake our small self-interested conclusions, our vulgar utilitarianism, for the truth. Like the Scottish student who was asked for an essay on elephants, we at once write at the top of the paper " The Elephant, its Economic Possibilities " ; without the slightest suspicion that this attitude towards the rich mystery of life is both blasphemous and absurd. For we have been shown the heavenly vision of the whole natural order, no less than the spiritual order, rising, growing and falling within the Holy Presence of God, supported and accompanied by the Creative Charity : and what is called the " Practice of the Presence of God," when we think of it in this fashion, calls for a very high level of loving admiration, self-oblivion, gentleness and faith—a certain child-like loyalty and humble awe, in the darkest moments as well as the best.

All this reminds us of the span and the depth which is required of a full Christian life of prayer. For one part of prayer associates us with that creative and supporting Love, and requires us to give ourselves as open channels through which it can be poured out on all life ; and the other part of prayer keeps us in humble awareness of our own complete dependence, plastic to the pressure of the moulding Charity. When we consider our situation like this, we realize that the very best we are likely to achieve in the world of prayer will be a small part in a mighty symphony ; not a peculiarly interesting duet. When our devotional life seems to us to have become a duet, we should listen more carefully. Then we shall hear a greater music, within which that little melody of ours can find its place.

This truth of the deep unity of creation links us with our lesser relations, and with our greater relations too. It makes us the members of a family, a social order, so rich and various that we can never exhaust its possibilities. " My little sisters, the birds," said St. Francis. " I am thy fellow-slave," said the great angel of the Apocalypse to the seer. We are all serving on one Staff. Our careful pickings and choosings, acceptances and exclusions, likes and dislikes, race prejudice, class prejudice, and all the rest, look rather silly within the glow of that One God, in Whom all live and move and have their being ; and the graduated splendour of that creation which is the work of His paternal Love. The Creed shows up human pride for the imbecility it is, and convinces us that realism is the same thing as humility. It insists upon our own utter dependence on the constant, varied, unseen Creative Love ; and the narrow span of our understanding of our fellow-creatures —how slight is the material we have for passing judgment on them—because our understanding is no wider than our charity.

And now we come down to the more painful consideration of all that this demands from us, if our inner and outer life are to match our belief about Reality ; and only when this has happened will Christianity conquer the world, harmonizing all things visible and invisible because both are received and loved as the works of One God. There are still far too many Christians in whose souls a sound-proof partition has been erected between the oratory and the kitchen : sometimes between the oratory and the study too. But the creative action of the Spirit penetrates the whole of life, and is felt by us in all sorts of ways. If our idea of that creative action is so restricted that we fail to recognize it working within the homely necessities and opportunities of our visible life, we may well suspect the quality of those invisible experiences to which we like to give spiritual status. " I found Him very easily among the pots and pans," said St. Teresa. " The duties of my position take precedence of everything else," said Elizabeth Leseur ; pinned down by those duties to a life which was a constant check on the devotional practices she loved. She recognized the totality of God's creative action, penetrating and controlling the whole web of life.

A genuine inner life must make us more and more sensitive to that moulding power, working upon His creation at every level, not at one alone : and especially to the constant small but expert touches, felt in and through very homely events, upon those half-made, unsteady souls which are each the subject of His detailed care. A real artist will give as much time and trouble to a miniature two inches square, as to the fresco on the Cathedral wall. The true splendour and heart-searching beauty of the Divine Charity is not seen in those cosmic energies which dazzle and confound us ; but in the transcendent power which stoops to an intimate and cherishing love, the grave and steadfast Divine action, sometimes painful and sometimes gentle, on the small unfinished soul. It is an unflickering belief in this, through times of suffering and conflict, apathy and desperation, in a life filled with prosaic duties and often empty of all sense of God, that the Creed demands of all who dare recite it.

We are so busy rushing about, so immersed in what we call practical things, that we seldom pause to realize the mysterious truth of our situation : how little · we know that really matters, how completely our modern knowledge leaves the deeps of our existence unexplored. We are inclined to leave all that out. But the Creed will not let us leave the mystery out. Christ never left it out. His teaching has a deep recurrent note of awe, a solemn sense of God and the profound mysteries of God : His abrupt creative entrance into every human life, coming to us, touching us, changing us in every crisis, grief, shock, sacrifice, flashing up on life's horizon like lightning just when we had settled down on the natural level, and casting over the landscape a light we had never dreamed of before. The whole teaching of Christ hinges on the deep mystery and awful significance of our existence ; and God, as the supreme and ever-present factor in every situation, from the tiniest to the most universal. The span of His understanding goes from the lilies of the field to the most terrible movements of history. He takes in all the darkness and anxiety of our situation, whether social or personal ; and within and beyond all, He finds the creative action of God, the one Reality, the one Life, working with a steadfast and unalterable love, sometimes by the direct action of circumstance and sometimes secretly within each soul in prayer. And this creative action, so hidden and so penetrating, is the one thing that matters in human life.

Jesus chose, as the most perfect image of that action, the working of yeast in dough. The leavening of meal must have seemed to ancient men a profound mystery, and yet something on which they could always depend. Just so does the supernatural enter our natural life, working in the hiddenness, forcing the new life into every corner and making the dough expand. If the dough were endowed with consciousness, it would not feel very comfortable while the yeast was working. Nor, as a rule, does our human nature feel very comfortable under the transforming action of God : steadily turning one kind of love into another kind of love, desire into charity, clutch into generosity, *Eros* into *Agape*. Creation is change, and change is often painful and mysterious to us. Spiritual creation means a series of changes, which at last produce Holiness, God's aim for men.

" O support me," says Newman, " as I proceed in this great, awful, happy change, with the grace of Thy unchangeableness. My unchangeableness, here below, is perseverance in changing." The inner life consists in an enduring of this deep transforming process. The chief object of prayer is to help it on : not merely for our own soul's sake, but for a reason which lifts the devotional life above all pettiness—because this is part of the great creative action which is lifting up humanity to the supernatural order, turning the flour and water of our common nature into the living Bread of Eternal Life. So, the first movement of our prayer must surely be a self-giving to this total purpose, whatever discipline and suffering it may involve for us.

It is a part of the great virtue of self-abandonment, to acknowledge the plain fact that God knows the recipe He is working from and the result He wants to obtain, and we do not. Some need the flame, and respond to its quick action. Others, like the cracknel, come to perfection by moving at a steady pace through the long dark oven which makes a perfect biscuit from a dab of paste. A generous acceptance of this ceaseless creative process, as the thing that matters most in human life, and a willingness to be transformed in whatever way is wanted and at whatever cost, unselfs the inner life, and makes it from the beginning accessible to the searching and delicate action of God ; working in ways of which we know nothing, entering and controlling every action, and using every creature, its efforts, sufferings and sacrifices, for the accomplishment of His hidden design.

In Paul Claudel's great play, " The Satin Slipper," the

whole of the action is made to depend on the single prayer of a dying missionary, left by pirates on a derelict ship. Bound to a spar as to a Cross, he offers up his death ; and so gives it the quality of a creative martyrdom, moves the secret springs of the spiritual world, and sets going a series of events which, after long years, save his brother's soul. The whole scene—the ship in the empty spaces of the Atlantic, the solitary man dying by inches, with the bodies of his companions piled up at his feet—looks to the world a frightful tragedy, a waste of noble lives. But the martyr himself takes it with great tranquillity, saying, " Doubtless the vintage could not come to pass without some disorder : but everything after a little stir, is gone back again into the great paternal peace." It is as if he said, " I believe in the Father Almighty, Creator of Heaven and earth, whose vision and love penetrate His whole creation ; and who deigns to use my small pain in the workshop of charity." Within this unseen spiritual order—which is, after all, the order into which we pass whenever we really pray—he gives with solemn joy his agony and death ; that so his brother, who will never know the price of his salvation, may be brought back to God. Twenty years later, the secret powers which his sacrifice released complete their work ; and by many crooked paths and strange places his brother's soul is brought to the feet of God.

Our entire confidence in that One God who is the Creator of all things, the Father of all His creation, and whose wisdom " sweetly orders " the working out of His undeclared design, must include such mysterious operations of grace as this. Again and again the sufferings of His children are made part of the yeast by which He changes and sanctifies all life. In our own inward life and prayer, this must mean a perpetual and peaceful self-offering for the hidden purposes of the Divine Charity, whatever they may be ; and especially the sacred privilege of giving a creative quality to all pain. This is perhaps what von Hügel had in mind, when he spoke of " getting our suffering well mixed up with our prayer." Only because he was a man of living prayer, and therefore humbly sensitive to the great movements of the world of spirit, could Claudel's missionary give creative power to his agony and death.

The same principle applies to our own daily existence. " The Kingdom of Heaven," the supernatural order, is like yeast. And we are required to be part of the Kingdom of Heaven : sons and daughters of God. That means that we too have our share in the creative process. We live and die within the workshop ; used as tools if we are merely dull and uninterested, but accepted as pupils and partners with our first movement of generosity in action, prayer or love. The implications of that truth must be worked out within each separate life : beginning where we are, content if our handful of meal can make a cottage loaf, not indulging spiritual vanity with large vague dreams about ovens full of beautiful brioches. Most of us when we were children managed sometimes to get into the kitchen ; a wonderful experience with the right kind of cook. A whole world separated the cook who let us watch her make the cake, from the cook who let us make a little cake of our own. Then we were filled with solemn interest, completely satisfied, because we were anticipating the peculiar privilege of human beings ; making something real, sharing the creative work of God. We, in our measure, are allowed to stand beside Him ; making little things, contributing our action to His great action on life. So we must use the material of life faithfully, with a great sense of responsibility; and especially our energy of prayer, with a due remembrance of its awful power.

William Blake has given us in two drawings his double vision of God, the Creator of all things. In the first, we see transcendent Intelligence and Will—the Ancient of Days—leaning out of heaven into chaos with the surveyor's compass in His hand, planning His mysterious universe: that vision of the Cosmic Mind to which science is now inclined to return. In the second drawing, one of Blake's most lovely inspirations, we see a Figure with outstretched arms and hidden face, driven down towards His dark world by the impetus of an unmeasured love, and encompassed and lit up by the flames of His own charity: and when we look more closely at this Figure, we see that there are wounds upon His hands and feet. With that revelation comes a great deepening and heightening of our experience, our belief, and our prayer. We add to the philosopher's concept of creation as the work of Divine Mind the saint's knowledge of creation as the work of Divine Charity; and of every soul stirred by that charity, however humble its individual part, as a fellow-worker with God.

CHAPTER III

ONE LORD

In the humility of thine infinite goodness, O God, thou dost show thyself as though thou were our creature, that thus thou mayest draw us unto thee.—*Nicolas of Cusa.*
The Word of God became visible to us through the Incarnation.—*St. Thomas Aquinas.*

AND now we turn from that overwhelming vision of a Creative Power and Love within us and above us, which is the Fact of facts for the religious soul, and we look at our own small lives and experiences : the confused material of everyday existence—with its social and personal demands, its ceaseless tension between natural and spiritual, mind and matter—with which we all have to deal. For it is there that we need so desperately the sanctifying presence of the Divine Charity, and there that it is so easily lost. There God must find us and abide with us, before we can ever find Him or abide with Him. And the next great Christian statement about Reality declares that this is what happens, and goes on happening all the time. " One Lord . . . God of God, Light of Light . . . who for us men and for our salvation came down from heaven." Of whom do we make this amazing statement ? We make it of the Divine Reason, the creative Thought of God, by whom all things are made. The Artist-Lover does not work on His creation from outside. The Absolute God, whom we can never escape but never comprehend, enters human life " not driven by necessity but drawn by Charity " and shows Himself to us in our own terms.

William Blake, in one of his great flashes of insight, said that there is in every human being two limits : Satan and Adam. Satan, the vigorous individualist, the self-adoring, self-sufficing creature, is the limit of what we can become under the steady action of self-will. His term of growth is that self-completion of which modern men are dreaming once more. He can give us all the kingdoms of this world. Already his submarines explore the deeps and his aeroplanes insult the heights. Adam, the unfinished, plastic creature, being made in the image of God, is slowly and tentatively producing under the steady action of the Divine Charity here one bit, and there another bit, of the Divine vision of perfect man : Christ our Brother. One way or another, we are all conscious of this two fold possibility in us, these two limits of animal and spiritual man ; one the fruit of self assertion, the other of docility. The inner life, at least in its early stages, is mainly realized as the tension between them. On one hand there is the steady, secret pressure of the yeast of grace, ever at work creating Adam, even though perhaps there is not much to show for it yet ; and the half-made creature struggling to breathe and to grow. On the other hand there is Satan, instinctive animal man, in command of all the lower centres of consciousness, aware of his own crude energy and holding on to his rights—the I, the Me, and the Mine. " All this will I give thee if thou wilt worship Me."

Who then is to rule in the house of life ? Who really sets the standard for humanity : animal man, the splendid creature with his instinct for dominance, intelligence and skill, or spiritual man, the strange, dependent, unfinished thing ? Christianity has no doubts about this. I believe in one Lord ; one supreme utterance of God within history, setting the standard, declaring the type. His Word, the expression of His Thought, speaks by means of one of His creatures, in a language we can understand, and says, " This is the truth about humanity ; this is what Adam is meant to be. I desire a creature made in My own image, the image of the Divine Charity : cleansed of all self-love and therefore capable of Infinite Love. So, I come to My own creatures, enter history in My mysterious being, My eternal reality, by means of a creature, Perfect Man : and show you what is meant by Infinite Love expressed in human terms."

This, of course, is what theology means by the Incarnation ; the eternal Charity of God finding utterance within His creation, and making of the common material of our earthly existence a revelation of His nature and so of the real nature of man. Divine Reality comes to us where we are, not as an " explanation " of our strange life—for this we could not understand—but as a direction how to live it ; and a very homely yet arduous direction too. " The Revelation of God," as Brunner has said, " is not a book or a doctrine but a living Person " : a person whose story and statements, in every point and detail, give us some deep truth about the life and will of that God who creates and sustains us, and about the power and vocation of a soul which is transformed in Him, and pays ungrudgingly the price of generous love. The " Mysteries " of Christ's earthly life, to give them their ancient name, have a beauty and truth of their own which lie on the surface, and which no one can miss. But this is nothing to the unfathomable truths which they reveal to those who contemplate them from within the world of prayer. They are like windows which break up the radiance of the Divine Charity into shapes and colours with which we can deal.

It sometimes happens that one goes to see a cathedral which is famous for the splendour of its glass; only to discover that, seen from outside, the windows give us no hint whatever of that which awaits us within. They all look alike; dull, thick, and grubby. From this point of view we already realize that they are ancient, important, the proper objects of reverence and study. But we cannot conceive that solemn coloured mystery, that richness of beauty, and meaning which is poured through them upon those who are inside the shrine. Then we open the door, and go inside. We leave the outer world and enter the inner world; and at once we are surrounded by a radiance, a beauty, that lie beyond the fringe of speech. The universal Light of God in which we live and move, and yet which in its reality always escapes us, pours through those windows; bathes us in an inconceivable colour and splendour, and shows us things of which we never dreamed before.

In the same way, the deep mysteries of the Being of God and the call of the soul cannot be seen by us, until they have passed through a human medium, a human life. Nor can that life, and all that it means as a revelation of God, His eternal truth and beauty, be realized by us from the outside. One constantly hears people commenting on Christianity, passing judgment on Christianity; and missing the point every time, because they are on the wrong side of the wall. It is only within the place of prayer, recollection, worship and love, the place where the altar is and where sacrifice is made, that we can cleanse our vision, overcome our self-interested bias, and fully and truly receive the revelation of Reality which is made to us in Christ.

There we begin to understand how every stage and

action of that life gives us something from beyond itself. It is like a series of windows, through which there streams into our human world the pure and life-giving light of the Eternal Charity, mediated to us in a way that we can bear ; so that " the eyes of the mind beholding the brightness of that splendour, by contemplating God made visible, we are caught up to the Invisible Love " as the ancient Preface for Christmas Day has it. Here Eternal Reality is given us in human terms ; convincing us of the reality of beauty, the reality of holiness, and the messy unreality of most of our own lives. Every time we re-enter that Cathedral of the Spirit, contemplate our Christian treasure from inside, we receive a fresh gift from its inexhaustible beauty and truth. As our humble receptiveness deepens and our eyes become more and more disciplined to that strange radiance, we see something we never noticed before ; penetrating, purifying and quickening us, enhancing our sense of the mystery and significance of our own life, its mingled homeliness and wonder. Yet all that we have so far seen is nothing to that which is still in reserve for us ; waiting for the cleansing and sanctification of our sight. Plato spoke of this life as a cave, in which men are imprisoned, only able to judge reality by the shadows which are cast by the light outside. But for Christians the cave—like some of those in which once the Pagan Mysteries were celebrated—has become a shrine. In that shrine we are shown truth pouring through the windows of holiness ; and are moulded for the true purpose of our creation, a life of charity, united to the self-giving generosity which is God.

For here, a Light we can bear to look at, and looking at must adore, comes to us from a Light we cannot bear to look at even whilst we worship it. The mystery of Reality enters history very gently by a human channel, and shows the character of Perfect Love within the life of man ; gives us something to hold on to, a Truth which is also a Way and a Life. What we see is not very sensational : but if we look at it steadily, it pierces the heart. First we see a baby, and a long hidden growth ; and then the unmeasured outpouring and self spending of an other-worldly love and mercy, teaching, healing, rescuing and transforming, but never trying to get anything for itself. And when we look deeper, we see beyond this a mysterious self-imparting, and a more mysterious anguish and struggle ; consummated at last in the most generous and lonely of deaths, issuing in a victory which has given life ever since to men's souls. Through this vivid life—what Christ does and how He does it, His prayer, His compassionate healing action, His use of suffering, His communion with God and man—the light of Reality floods our twilit inner lives ; showing us the human transfigured by the Divine. This is what St. Ignatius Loyola intended and desired when he taught his pupils to " contemplate the Mysteries of the Life of Christ." Few people do it properly. They are too anxious to get on and be practical : for the lesson of the one thing needful is a lesson which human nature instinctively resists. Yet we shall make our own small work of art all the better if we soak our souls in that beauty first.

This simple contemplation of Christ is a very important part of the life of prayer : for we receive spiritual truth far more by absorption than by exploration, moreover, that which we see has a direct bearing on our own inner life, which is required to conform to the pattern here disclosed to us. Again and again the mystics have insisted that every homely incident of this story has a precise and immortal meaning for the spirit of man. Historical religion only matters because it shows us something happening on the stage of this world, which is eternally happening and eternally true in the spiritual world. The cycle of growth from the Manger to the Cross must take place in every soul ; and every soul must be subdued to the teaching, healing and transfiguring action of the Word on the plastic raw material of human personality. Nothing is there by accident. No stage or phase can be left out : for here " God speaks in a Son," the very substance of the Holy, incarnate by the action of that Spirit who is the Giver of all life. Thus in our struggle to express even our fragmentary vision of God's purpose, we are forced to pass backwards and forwards between the different aspects of His self-giving love. Christian belief in its richness can never rest long in one alone. When Prudence was catechizing little James in the House of the Interpreter, she expressed great satisfaction because that remarkably theological child insisted that he was both made and saved by the whole Trinity. And perhaps deeper meditation on the splendour of our faith in its wholeness might indeed enlighten our eyes, to behold anew the Charity of that God Who reveals Himself supremely by hiding Himself in humanity : uttering His Word within history so that we His creatures, living historical lives in space and time, may meet the Holy there as at once our Brother and our Lord.

When we consider the heavens, and the awful vistas which science reveals to us, and then contemplate this generosity—so searching in its tenderness, and so passing knowledge in its energy, that mere religious sentiment wilts when it draws near and " practical Christianity " is beaten to its knees—then before this lowly and yet sublime self-giving of the Very Godhead to its creation, we are surely forced to some faint reflection of that same charity in our turn. For this deep and searching process points to something far beyond the mere improvement of this world and its conditions, or the mere comfort of our own little souls. God in His essential Being is Charity ; God so loved that He gave ; therefore to dwell in Charity means giving in our turn, a movement of unconditioned generosity which shall be the expression of love. The human soul cuts rather a ridiculous figure, clutching its own bit of luggage, its private treasures, its position, its personality, its rights, over against the holy self-giving of Absolute Love manifest in the flesh. That strange and glimmering Presence, standing on the frontier between the divine and human worlds, attracting and convicting us, asks a total and flexible self-offering as the only possible attitude of man. " Christ's human nature," says the *Theologia Germanica*, " was so utterly emptied of self and all creatures that it was nothing else but the house, the habitation, the possession of God." Only thus could the celestial wisdom enter our life ; and the conditions are still the same.

" Who for us men and our salvation came down." Why ? So that we could know something about Holiness. For no amount of description really tells us anything about Holiness ; but an encounter with it shames, amazes, convinces and delights us all at once. " Thou art the Christ ! " says St. Peter. " My Lord and my God ! " says St. Thomas. They recognize something from beyond the world : One who enters our mixed life in His perfect beauty ; and accepts all the normal conditions of an existence which is so much at the mercy of seasons and weather, thirst and hunger, so afflicted by distresses we do not understand, so vexed by devils we cannot cast out

D

and tainted by sins we cannot forget.   Through all this that Figure is walking ; radiating in and through every situation a selfless charity, an untiring interest and love.   The Word has spoken ; and spoken in the language of everyday life.   And because of this, within that everyday life man always has access to God ; and can never, at any point in his career claim ignorance of the drift of God's Will, even though his own duty and action may often be hard to decide.   God is Charity ; and the human race has one Lord, who is Incarnate Charity and carries through its utmost demands to the Altar and the Cross.   Every decision, therefore, that the Christian takes in life will be controlled by the fact that it must be compatible with following Him. This means that no Christian life will avoid Calvary ; though we may come to it by many different ways.

So, because Holiness has entered our world, and appeared in our nature, we know that men and women can become holy ; and are bound, in spite of all discouragements, to take an optimistic view of human life.   The Church is an undying family which has its face set towards Holiness, and is fed upon the food which can—if we let it —produce Holiness.   As the queen bee is produced by being fed from childhood on " royal jelly," and thus becomes the parent of new life ; so it is what the Christian is given, and what he assimilates of the supernatural food—not what he is by nature—which makes him grow up into the life-giving order of God.   The final test of holiness is not seeming very different from other people, but being used to make other people very different ; becoming the parent of new life.

It is true that before this happens we must ourselves be changed ; must absorb the " royal jelly," feed on the Divine Charity.   The saints are there to show us that this is a practical necessity, not a devotional day-dream. Their lives disclose to us in all its delicacy and perfection God's creative action in the realm of soul. As we enter into those transformed and sacrificial lives—some of them so near in time and place to our own—we see what it really means to have one Lord. It means everything else in life subordinated to this one fact : no exceptions. It means Francis Xavier and David Livingstone travelling for Him to the ends of the earth, and Father Wainright living for Him for half a century in one slum ; Bunyan going to prison for Him, and Francis de Sales and Fénelon going to Court for Him ; Mary Slessor ruling in the jungle and Julian of Norwich hidden in the anchoress' cell ; Elizabeth Fry facing the criminals in Newgate gaol and Josephine Butler facing the shocked hostility of Victorian piety ; Elizabeth Leseur accepting a painful and limited life, Charles de Foucauld going out into great spaces and dying alone in the desert with his love.

What follows from all this ? What follows—and the saints show it to us again and again in the various beauty of their lives—is that we are not required to go outside the frame of normal experience in order to fulfil the creative design of God for souls. There is no place and no career which lies outside Eternity, and cannot incarnate something of the Eternal Charity. What was done in the carpenter's shop can be done in the engineer's shop too. " Perfect God and perfect Man " is a formula which endorses our ordinary human life, even in its most forbidding phases, as fully adequate to the demands of spiritual life ; so long as that human life really has one Lord. It matters little that the stable gives way before the garage, the temple before the church, or that hydroplanes alight on the Sea of Galilee.

This is surely an important truth for us. It shows that there need be no separation, no forced option between our life of action and our life of prayer. In the saints, the action and the prayer are mixed together, and make something quite concrete. " The mirage shall become a pool !" says Isaiah. The lovely glowing dream seen in our meditations becomes a genuine reality, a source of living water for the thirsty, when we find ourselves in the disconcerting presence of a saint. There are plenty of spiritual systems which show us the beautiful mirage. Only in Christianity does it become a pool, a reservoir of living water to refresh our thirsty world.

So " I believe in one Lord . . . incarnate," with all that lies between, means " I believe in the Divine Charity which is Reality, self-revealed in human nature and among the normal surroundings of men. And further, because of this I believe in the possibility of my nature being so transformed by the creative action of the Spirit, that it may become part of the Mystical Body through which that revelation goes on ; for the Divine Charity is still pressing into life through our narrow souls, seeking to bring in the Kingdom of God. Therefore my whole life, physical, intellectual and spiritual must be governed by this fact: by my trust in the unlimited power of God to remake me here and now—in my present environment, however unpromising it looks—and by an absolute, generous willingness to co-operate with Him, however much it hurts. Every event, situation, joy or contradiction can be so dealt with that it strengthens either the rule of Charity within the soul or the rule of self-love. All depends on whether attention is focussed on the great purposes of God, or our own small purposes ; even those small purposes to which we like to give spiritual rank.

For however harmless and legitimate those personal aims may seem to be, they lie under suspicion if they do not incarnate something of the spirit of self-imparting Love.

PART II

CHAPTER IV

INCARNATE

Thy holy life is our way, and by holy patience we walk to thee, who art our head and governor. And if thou, Lord, hadst not gone before and showed us the way, who would have endeavoured to have followed ?—*Thomas à Kempis.*

Then thought I with myself, who that goeth on pilgrimage, but would have one of these maps about him, that he may look, when he is at a stand, which is the way he must take.—*The Pilgrim's Progress.*

NOT long ago, I was standing in an artist's studio before an altar-piece which she had just made. It represented the Nativity : or rather, the eternal incarnation of the Holy, self-given for the world. In the foreground one saw the Blessed Virgin, its ordained instrument, and St. Joseph, watching by her bed. There was a patient grave simplicity about them both ; reflected in the serious young angels, whose majestic scale suggested the greatness of that world of spirit from which they had been drawn. Below, the sheep were feeding very quietly too : innocent nature entirely at home among the mysteries of the supernatural order, one lamb turning from its mother to press more closely to the Mother of the Lamb of God. And behind the Blessed Virgin, the focus of the mystery, the link as it were between two worlds, the Child lay peacefully and helplessly on a small stone altar, as on a bed. The stillness of an eternal event brooded over the whole. I spoke to the artist of the beauty of this ancient conception ; and she answered, " Yes, laid on the altar straight away. I like that. There's something so sturdy about it."

Our modern religion hardly makes enough of this element in the mystery of the Divine revelation; in His pattern declared to humanity, or in the life of prayer. Yet sturdiness, shouldering the burden and accepting the tension inevitable to all great undertakings—getting to grips with the dread problems of life, and the cost of all redemptive action—comes nearer than any fervour to the Mind of Christ, and the demands of Charity. It is comparatively easy for devout minds to feel moved, contrite, exalted, adoring; much more difficult to discount all feeling, and be sturdy about it. Christ was trained in a carpenter's shop; and we persist in preferring a confectioner's shop. But the energy of rescue, the outpouring of sacrificial love, which the supernatural life demands, is not to be got from a diet of devotional meringues and éclairs. The whole life made an oblation from the first—placed on the altar, and lived right through as a reasonable sacrifice from beginning to end—this is the pattern put before us. Only thus can humanity use to the full its strange power of embodying eternal realities; and uniting the extremes of mystery and homeliness.

Nothing in this story, perhaps, is more significant than the quietness and simplicity of its beginning. The birth of the Child, the Shepherds and the Magi, the little boy of Nazareth and his wonderful experience in the Temple, and the long quiet years in the carpenter's shop; there seems at first sight nothing very supernatural in these things. Indeed, one of the most convicting aspects of Christianity, if we try to see it in terms of our own day, is the contrast between its homely and inconspicuous beginnings and the holy powers it brought into the world. It keeps us in perpetual dread of despising small things, humble people, little groups. The Incarnation means that the Eternal God enters our common human life with all the energy of His creative love, to transform it, to exhibit to us its richness, its unguessed significance ; speaking our language, and showing us His secret beauty on our own scale.

Thus the spiritual life does not begin in an arrogant attempt at some peculiar kind of other-worldliness, a rejection of ordinary experience. It begins in the humble recognition that human things can be very holy, full of God ; whereas high-minded speculations about His nature need not be holy at all. Since all life is engulfed in Him, He can reach out to us anywhere and at any level. The depth and richness of His Eternal Being are unknown to us. Yet Christianity declares that this unsearchable Life, which is in essence a self-giving Love, and is wholly present wherever it loves, so loved this world as to desire to reveal within it the deepest secret of His thought ; appearing within and through His small, fugitive, imperfect creatures, in closest union with humanity. In the beginning was the Word : and the Word was God, and without Him was not anything made that hath been made : and the Word became flesh and dwelt among us.

That seems immense. A complete philosophy is contained in it. And then we come down to the actual setting of this supreme event, and at once all our notions of the suitable and the significant are set aside ; all our pet values reversed. A Baby, just that ; and moreover, a Baby born in the most unfortunate circumstances. The extremes of the transcendent and the homely are suddenly brought together in this disconcerting revelation of reality. The hard life of the poor, its ceaseless preoccupation with the lowliest of human needs and duties, the absolute surrender and helplessness, the half-animal status of babyhood; all this is the chosen vehicle for the unmeasured inpouring of the Divine Life and Love. So too the strange simplicity of its beginning both rebukes and reassures us. It is like a quiet voice speaking in our deepest prayer : " The Lord is with thee " . . . and calling forth the one and only answer, " Behold the handmaid of the Lord, be it unto me according to thy Word ! " Humble self-abandonment is found and declared to be enough to give us God. First in one way and then in another, all the incidents which cluster round the mystery of the Incarnation seem designed to show us this; the simplest yet the deepest truth about His relation to the soul.

Look for instance at the story of the Magi : those scholars of the ancient world, turning from their abstruse calculations and searching of the heavens because they saw a new star, and driven to seek along fresh paths for a clue to the mystery of life. What they found does not seem at first sight what we should now call " intellectually satisfying." It was not a revelation of the Cosmic Mind, but a poor little family party ; yet there they were brought to their knees—because, like the truly wise, they were really humble-minded—before a little, living, growing thing. The utmost man can achieve on his own here capitulates before the unspeakable and mysterious simplicity of the method of God; His stooping down to us, His self-disclosure at the very heart of life. After all, the shepherds got there long before the Magi ; and even so, the animals were already in position when the shepherds arrived. He comes to His own ; the God of our natural life makes of that natural life the very material of His self-revelation. His smile kindles the whole universe ; His hallowing touch lies upon all life. The animal world and the natural world have their own rights and their own place within the Thought of God. There never was a religion more deeply in touch with natural things than Christianity, although it is infinite in its scope.

The essence of the story of the Magi is that it is no use to be too clever about life. Only in so far as we find God in it, do we find any meaning in it. Without Him it is a tissue of fugitive and untrustworthy pleasures, desires, conflicts, frustrations and intolerable pains. Historical Christianity need not involve for us an elaborate philosophy of the Spirit : but it does mean accepting as deeply significant all the great events of the Gospel, because conveying God. And, if we thus recognize the supernatural within these events, some so strange and some so homely ; then, we also accept all these incidents as carrying a sacramental reference, conveying something of the over-ruling will and thought of God, and having something in them for each of us. If we are ever to learn all that this record can mean for us, we must never forget that these beyond all other facts of history, are indwelt and moulded by the Divine Charity, are plastic to His creative thought. Everything is there because it conveys spiritual truth in human ways ; is a part of all we mean by Incarnation. It all " speaks to our condition," as George Fox would say. The Synoptic Gospels may not always have the accuracy of a photograph ; but they have a higher realism, because they are charged with God. Like some great work of art, they give us more and more light and food, reveal greater depths of significance, as we grow in that wisdom which is the child of humility and love. That is why meditation on the Christian mysteries, chewing the cud of the Gospels, is so nourishing to the soul, and so inexhaustible as a basis of prayer.

The story of the Magi shows the new life which has appeared within the rich texture of our normal experience, casting its purifying radiance upon the whole existence of man : the Light of the world, not the sanctuary lamp of a well-appointed church. Cosy religious exclusiveness is condemned in this mystery. It is easy for the pious to join the shepherds, and feel in place at the Crib, and look out into the surrounding darkness saying, " Look at those extraordinary intellectuals wandering about after a star ; they seem to have no religious sense. Look what curious gifts and odd types of self-consecration they are bringing ; not at all the sort of people one sees in church." Yet the child who began by receiving those unexpected pilgrims had a woman of the streets for His most faithful friend, and two thieves for His comrades at the last. Looking at these extremes, so deeply significant of the Christian spirit, we can learn something, perhaps, of the height and depth and breadth of that divine generosity into which our narrow and fragmentary loves must be absorbed. It was said of Father Wainright that he cared above all for the scamp, the drunkard and the outsider, least of all for those who came regularly to church ; and no man of our time has been fuller of the Spirit of Christ. The Epiphany means the free pouring out of a limitless light—the Light of the World—not its careful communication to those whom we hold worthy to receive it. The Magi, after all, took more trouble than the shepherds. They came a longer journey, by more perilous paths. The intellectual virtues and longings of men are all blessed in Christ, " the intellectual radiance full of love."

We turn to another point which every mystery in its turn will show us ; for they are there to light up the cycle of our own interior growth. In our souls too the Divine

Charity must be incarnate; take visible, tangible form. We are not really Christians until this has been done. The Eternal Birth, says Eckhart, must take place in you. And another mystic says that human nature is like a stable, inhabited by the ox of passion and the ass of prejudice; animals which take up a lot of room, and which I suppose that most of us are feeding on the quiet. It is there, between them, pushing them out of the way, that the Divine Child is to be born, and in their very manger He will be laid: and they will be the first to fall down before Him. Sometimes Christians seem far nearer to those animals than to the child in His simple poverty and self-abandonment. And here again, God's mysterious and life-giving action in the soul is for a purpose that points beyond ourselves. It happens not merely for our sakes; but because His manifestation to the world must be through us. Every real Christian is part of the dust-laden air which shall radiate the glowing Charity of God; catch and reflect His golden light. Ye are the light of the world, because you are irradiated by the one Light of the World, the holy generosity of God. The great New Testament saints—in fact, all saints—look right through and past the outward appearance of men's lives, and seek only for the seed of the divine life within them, the hidden Child of God. " Ye are of God, little children," exclaims St. John " greater is He that is in you than he that is in the world." That is the awful truth which rules the inner life of man.

And now we turn from the central mystery to the clustered events, through which its character is disclosed. We see the new life growing in secret. Nothing very startling happens. We see the child in the carpenter's workshop. He does not go outside the frame of the homely life in which He appeared. It did quite well for Him, and will do quite well for us ; there is no need for peculiar conditions in order to grow in the spiritual life, for the pressure of God's Spirit is present everywhere and at all times. Our environment itself, our home and our job, is the medium through which we experience His moulding action and His besetting love. It is not Christian to try and get out of our frame, or separate our outward life from our life of prayer, since both are the creation of one Charity. The third-rate little town in the hills, with its limited social contacts and monotonous manual work, reproves us when we begin to fuss about our opportunities and our scope. And this quality of quietness, ordinariness, simplicity, with which the saving action of God enters history, endures from the beginning to the end. The child grows like other children, and the lad works like other lads : there is a total abandonment of the individual to the vast Divine purpose, working at its own pace and through ordinary life, and often to us in mysterious ways.

We must surely believe that much in Christ's own destiny was deeply mysterious to Him. It seems part of a completed manhood, that He shared our strange human situation, our entire dependence, in this too. The New Testament narrative, with its emphasis on moments when the clouds parted, and He saw His call and what was at work in Him seems to suggest by contrast other, longer stretches ; when He looked out from His earthly tabernacle on no clear view, but a path to be trodden in pure abandonment to God. Here again our interior life is conformed to the same pattern. In a general way we must go on steadily, without presuming to demand a clear view. We cannot break the cloud of unknowing in which our lives are folded : like Nicodemus, we must come to Him by night. This should make us realize how deeply hidden, how

gradual and unseen by us, the soul's growth in the life of
prayer is likely to be. It is like the hidden life at Nazareth.
We must be content with the wholesome routine of the
nursery, doing ordinary things, learning ordinary lessons
and eating ordinary food, if we are to grow truly and or-
ganically in wisdom and stature and favour with God and
man. Growth in God is a far more gradual, less conscious
process than we realize at first. We are so raw and super-
ficial in our notions, that we cannot conceive the nature of
those tremendous changes by which the child of grace
becomes the man of God. We all want to be up and doing
long before we are ready to do.

To contemplate the proportions of Christ's life is a
terrible rebuke to spiritual impatience and uppish hurry.
There we see how slow, according to our time-span, is the
maturing of the thought of God. Ephemeral insects become adult in a few minutes, the new-born lamb gets up
and starts grazing straight away, but the child depends for
months on its mother's love. Sanctity, which is childhood
in God, partakes of the long divine duration. We often
feel that we ought to get on quickly, reach a new stage of
knowledge or prayer, like spiritual may-flies. But Christ's
short earthly life is divided into thirty years for growth
and two and a half for action. The pause, the hush, the
hiddenness, which intervenes between the Birth and the
Ministry, is part of the divine method, and an earnest of
the greatness of that which is to come. Only when that
quiet growth has reached the right stage is there a revelation of God's purpose, and the stress and discipline of a
crucial choice. Baptism, Fasting and Temptation come
together as signs of maturity. It is much the same with
us in the life of prayer. The Spirit fills us as we grow and
make room. It keeps pace with us; does not suddenly

E

stretch us like a pneumatic tyre, with dangerous results.
To contemplate the life of Christ, said St. Augustine,
"cures inflation, and nourishes humility." We see in
Him the gradual action of God, subdued to the material on
which it works, and fostering and sanctifying growth—
that holy secret process—especially growth in the hidden,
interior life, which is the unique source of His power in us.

All gardeners know the importance of good root
development before we force the leaves and flowers. So
our life in God should be deeply rooted and grounded
before we presume to expect to produce flowers and fruits ;
otherwise we risk shooting up into one of those lanky
plants which can never do without a stick. We are constantly beset by the notion that we ought to perceive ourselves springing up quickly, like the seed on stony ground ;
show striking signs of spiritual growth. But perhaps we
are only required to go on quietly, making root, growing
nice and bushy ; docile to the great slow rhythm of life.
When we see no startling marks of our own religious progress or our usefulness to God, it is well to remember the
baby in the stable and the little boy in the streets of
Nazareth. The very life was there present, which was to
change the whole history of the human race ; the rescuing
action of God. At that stage there was not much to show
for it ; yet there is perfect continuity between the stable
and the Easter garden, and the thread that unites them is
the hidden Will of God. The childish prayer of Nazareth
was the right preparation for the awful prayer of the Cross.

So it is that the life of the Spirit is to unfold gently and
steadily within us ; till at the last the full stature for which
God designed us is attained. It is an organic process, a
continuous Divine action ; not a sudden miracle or a
series of jerks. Therefore there should be no struggle,

impatience, self-willed effort in our prayer and self-discipline; but rather a great flexibility, a homely ordered life, a gentle acceptance of what comes to us, and a still gentler acceptance of the fact that much we see in others is still out of our own reach. The prayer of the growing spirit should be free, humble, simple; full of confidence and full of initiative too. The mystics constantly tell us, that the goal of this prayer and of the hidden life which shall itself become more and more of a prayer, is union with God. We meet this phrase often: far too often, for we lose the wholesome sense of its awfulness. What does union with God mean? Not a nice feeling which we enjoy in devout moments. This may or may not be a by-product of union with God; probably not. It can never be its substance. Union with God means such an entire self-giving to the Divine Charity, such identification with its interests, that the whole of our human nature is transformed in God, irradiated by His absolute light, His sanctifying grace. Thus it is woven up into the organ of His creative activity, His redeeming purpose; conformed to the pattern of Christ, heart, soul, mind and strength. Each time this happens, it means that one more creature has achieved its destiny; and each soul in whom the life of the Spirit is born, sets out towards that goal.

If men and women want to know what this means in terms of human nature and human experience, one sovereign way is offered them; the contemplation of Christ's life. There we see that we are not to grow in wisdom and stature for our own sakes, in order to achieve what is really a self-interested spirituality. The growth is for a reason that points beyond ourselves: in order that the teaching, healing, life-changing power of the Divine Charity may possess us, and work through us. We must lose our own lives, in order to be possessed by that life : that unmeasured Divine generosity which enters the human world in such great humility, as the Infinite Light pours through narrow lancets, conformed to our human limitations, growing at our human pace. The Holy Child sets up a standard for both the simple and the learned ; teaching a great simplicity and self-oblivion, a willingness and readiness to respond to life wherever we may find it, and to grow and change, not according to our preconceived ideas of pace and method, but according to the overruling will and pace of God.

CHAPTER V

CRUCIFIED

Truth is to be worshipped, though it hang naked on a Cross.—
St. Bruno.

The mystery revealed, in a unique degree and form, in Christ's life, is really a universal spiritual-human law ; the law of suffering and sacrifice, as the one way to joy and possession, which has existed, though veiled till now, since the foundation of the world.—
F. von Hügel.

A CHRISTIAN'S belief about reality is a wonderful blend of confidence and experience. On one hand it asks great faith in the invisible world that enfolds us. On the other hand it includes and embraces the hardest facts of the actual life we know, and gives them a creative quality. It is a religion which leaves nothing out. After the great phrases in which the Creed tries to describe or suggest the eternal Divine Nature, and the mystery of that Infinite God disclosing Himself in and through His creatures—incarnate by the action of the Holy Spirit of Charity—it goes on to a series of plain statements about the life of Christ. He was born, a baby ; made man ; entered completely into our human situation. He was crucified at a particular moment in the history of a particular country, suffered, was buried, and rose again to a new quality of life. This sequence of facts, deliberately picked out as specially significant moments in the revelation of Divine Charity to us, is not merely a series of symbolic or spiritual events. These things, on their surface so well known—but in their deep significance and bearing on life so carefully ignored by us—happened in time and space to a real man, a real body ; of flesh and nerve and bone, accessible to all the demands of our physical nature and all the humiliations of physical pain. To the world He merely appeared a local prophet of somewhat limited appeal ; yet endowed with the strange power of healing and transforming all lives given into His hand. Having roused the hostility of official religion by His generous freedom of love, He was condemned by a combination of political cowardice and ecclesiastical malice to a barbarous and degrading death ; and made of that death the supreme triumph of self-abandoned Charity.

Yet as we meditate on these familiar facts, and recollect that in and through them the One God in whom we believe is self-revealed to man's soul, we are gradually aware of a light which comes through them, and shames us by its disclosure of what a perfected human nature might be, and is therefore intended to be. *Lumen Christi.* The Light of the World enters our life to show us reality ; and forces us to accept the fact that it is the whole of that life, not some supposed spiritual part of it, which is involved in our response to God, and must be self-given to the mysterious purposes of Charity. Christianity is a religion which concerns us as we are here and now, creatures of body and soul. We do not " follow the footsteps of His most holy life " by the exercise of a trained religious imagination ; but by treading the firm rough earth, up hill and down dale, on the mountain, by the lake-side, in garden, temple, street, or up the strait way to Calvary. The whole physical scene counts and is of vital importance to Christians ; it can and does test us, save us or break us. So, to dismiss the pressures, limitations and crucial problems of practical life, bodily sufferings and self-denials, or even the most childlike and crude devotional exercises, as merely material, merely external, and so on, witnesses to a cheap and fundamentally unchristian attitude of mind ; a complete misunderstanding of our real situation and the many-levelled richness of God's revelation within life. " Dear Wood, dear Iron ! " says the great hymn of the Cross, with relentless realism, " Dear the Weight that hung on thee ! "

Human beings are saved by a Love which enters and shares their actual struggle, darkness and bewilderment, their subjection to earthly conditions. By a supreme exercise of humility the deep purposes of God are worked out through man's natural life with all its powers, humiliations, conflicts and sufferings, its immense capacity for heroic self-giving, disinterested love ; not by means of ideas, insights, and spiritual experiences even of the loftiest kind. Charity, generosity, accepting the vocation of sacrifice, girding itself with lowliness as one that serveth and then going straight through with it, suffering long, never flinching, never seeking its own, discloses its sacred powers to us within the arena of our homely everyday existence : and it is by the varied experiences and opportunities of that daily existence, that our dull and stubborn nature shall be trained for the glorious liberty of eternal life.

The Word, the Thought of God, made flesh and dwelling among us, accepted our conditions, did not impose His. He took the journey we have to take, with the burden we have to carry. We cannot then take refuge in our unfortunate heredity, temperament, or health when faced by the demands of the spiritual life. It is as complete human beings, taught and led by a complete Humanity, that we respond to the pressure of God. The saints carried the burdens of heredity, temperament, and health. It is no easy amiability which we see transformed to the purpose of Creative Love in St. Paul or St. Augustine. St. Catherine of Genoa had no natural gift of joy, or St. Francis Xavier of humility. Bunyan and Fox knew conflicts as bitter as our own. These are they that came out of much tribulation. There are other forms of saving tribulation than martyrdom, many ways of enduring to the end; but none that does not involve the painful conflict between softness and sturdiness, natural self-love and supernatural divine love. Grace does not work *in vacuo* : it works on the whole man, that many-levelled creature ; and shows its perfect work in One who is described as Very Man, and of whom we cannot think without the conflict of Gethsemane and the surrender of the Cross.

Since, then, the career which begins upon the altar as a living sacrifice to the purposes of Charity, and works out this sublime vocation to the bitter end, is to be the pattern of the Christian's inner life, there must always be something in this life which is the equivalent of the Passion and the Cross. Suffering has its place within the Divine purpose, and is transfigured by the touch of God. A desperate crisis, the demand for a total self-giving, a willingness to risk everything, an apparent failure, darkness and death —all these are likely to be incidents of a spiritual course. Those who complain that they make no progress in the life of prayer because they " cannot meditate " should examine, not their capacity for meditation, but their capacity for suffering and love. For there is a hard and costly element, a deep seriousness, a crucial choice in all genuine religion, of which the New Testament warns us on every page ; and this is more and more made plain to us as we leave its surface and penetrate to its solemn deeps. There we find a suffering and love twined so closely together, that we cannot wrench them apart : and if we try to do so, the love is maimed in the process—loses its creative power—and the suffering remains, but without its aureole of willing sacrifice.

Love, after all, makes the whole difference between an execution and a martyrdom. Pain, or at least the willingness to risk pain, alone gives dignity to human love, and is the price of its creative power : without this, it is mere emotional enjoyment. It costs much to love any human being to the bitter end ; and on every plane a total generosity, a love that includes pain and embraces it, is the price of all genuine achievement. The son of man must suffer, in the last desperate conflict between supernatural self-giving and natural self-love. The Cross means the ultimate helplessness and dependence of man, when he comes up to his own limit and has nothing left but charity ; and his willing acceptance of that helplessness and limit, because it throws him back upon the God he trusts and loves. So here, by the Crucifix and what it means to them, Christians must test their position. What we really think about the Cross means, ultimately, what we really think about life. It stands upon the frontier of two worlds ; the final test of humanity's worth. " Seek where you will," says Thomas a Kempis, "everywhere you will find the Cross." When you have found it, what are you going to do about it ? That is the supreme question which decides our spiritual destiny. Are we merely to look at it with horror, or accept it with adoration and gratitude, as the soul's unique chance of union with the Charity of God ?

It has been said that the whole of Christ's life was a Cross. I think that saying does grave injustice to its richness of response ; the real joy and beauty of His contacts with nature, children, friends, the true happiness we find in the saints nearest to Him, the hours snatched for the deeply satisfying prayer of communion, the outburst of rejoicing when He discerns the Father's will. The span of perfect manhood surely includes and ratifies all this. But it was the deep happiness of the entirely self-abandoned, giving without stint truth, health and rescue, and always at His own cost : not the easy, shallow satisfaction of those who live to express themselves. There is a marked contrast between the first phase of the Ministry, with its confident movement within the natural world—healing what is wrong in it, and using what is right in it, and sharing with simplicity the social life of men—and the second phase, from the Transfiguration to the end. Then, we get a sense of increasing conflict with that same world, and the growing conviction that what is so deeply wrong with it can only be mended by a love that is expressed in sacrifice. The Suffering Servant, bearing its griefs and carrying its sorrows, is the one who most perfectly conveys the Divine Charity, and serves his brethren best.

" If anyone would come after Me, let him take up the Cross." The spiritually natural life is very charming and the exclusively spiritual life is very attractive. But both stop short of that unconditioned self-giving, that willing entrance into the world's sufferings and confusion which God asks of rescuing souls. It was in the Passion, says St. John of the Cross, that Christ " accomplished that supreme work which His whole life, its miracles and works of power, had not accomplished—the union and reconciliation of human nature with the life of God." Here we learn what it really means to volunteer for the Christian life.

The first movement of His soul was self-donation to the purposes of the Father. " I must be about my Father's business." It seems the most lovely, most privileged, of vocations at that point. The last movement of His soul was the utter self-giving of the Cross : " Father, into Thy Hands I commend my spirit " ; the perfection of self-oblivious love. That is the true culmination of the story which began with the child of Bethlehem. It is a very lop-sided revelation of love which gives us the Manger without the Cross. They are like two windows standing North and South of that altar where the Divine Life is eternally self-given to men.

"We are made partakers of Christ," says the writer of *Hebrews*, " if we hold the beginning of our confidence steadfast to the end." The beginning is easy and lovely. It is the end that tests to the utmost our courage and love. " Can you drink of My cup and be baptized with My baptism ? " Not unless you care far more about God and His purposes than you do about your own soul ; but that is the very essence of a spiritual life. Profound submission to the Will of God declared through circumstances : being what we are, and the world what it is, that means sooner or later Gethsemane, and the Cross, and the darkness of the Cross. Most of the saints have been through that. We do not begin to understand the strange power of the Passion, the light it casts on existence, till we see what it was in their lives.

For union with the Cross means experience of the dread fact of human nature, that only those who are willing to accept suffering up to the limit are capable of giving love up to the limit ; and that this is the only kind of love which can be used for the purposes of the redeeming life. It is on Good Friday, and only then, that the ancient liturgies hail Christ as the Strong, the Holy, the Immortal ; as if this crisis alone could disclose in its fulness His mysterious power. And it is at the Institution of the Eucharist, on the eve of that apparent failure, that they place in His mouth the words of the Psalmist, " The right hand of the Lord bringeth mighty things to pass ! I shall not die but live, and declare the works of the Lord ! " Every Christian altar witnesses to that. The living power of Christ within the world, the Food He gives eternally to men, have been won by the costly exercise of a heroic love.

In the chapter-house of S. Marco at Florence, the artist-saint, Fra Angelico, has painted the patrons of the city and the founders of the great religious orders—dedicated servants of the Eternal Charity—adoring the Crucified who is their Pattern, and from whom their mandate comes. There they are : real human beings of every type, transfigured by a single costly loyalty. There is Mark, the self-effacing writer of the earliest Gospel. There is the Magdalen, completely sanctified by penitence and love. There are the holy women, whose service was of the homeliest kind. There are Cosmo and Damian, the good and honest physicians. There too are the devoted scholars, Jerome and Augustine ; and Benedict, the creator of an ordered life of work and prayer. There are Francis, lost in an ecstacy of loving worship, and Thomas Aquinas gazing at the key to that great Mystery of Being to which he had given his vast intellectual powers. All these— mystics, lovers, teachers, scholars, workers—are linked with the Crucified, the Holy and Self-given, whose agents they are and from whom they draw power and love. The whole range of human accomplishment, in these its chosen representatives, is shown to us in direct and glad dependence on the ever-flowing Charity of God. That is the very substance of religion. Like an immense impetus of generosity, it pours out from the Heart of Reality ; self-given through generous and adoring spirits of every sort and kind, to rescue and transform the world.

If then we look at the Crucifix—" that supreme symbol of our august religion," as von Hügel loved to call it—and then at our selves, testing by the Cross the quality of our courage and love; if we do this honestly and unflinchingly, this will be in itself a complete self-examination, judgment, purgatory. It is useless to talk in a large vague way about the Love of God. Here is its point of insertion in the world of men, in action, example and demand. Every Christian is required to be an instrument of God's rescuing action; and His power will not be exerted through us except at considerable cost to ourselves. Muzzy, safety-first Christianity is useless here. We must accept the world's worst if we are to give it of our best. The stinging lash of humiliation and disillusionment, those unfortunate events which strip us of the seamless robe of convention and reserve, and expose us naked to the world in the weakness of our common humanity, the wounds given by those we love best, the revelation that someone we had trusted could not be trusted any more, and the peculiar loneliness and darkness inseparable from some phases of the spiritual life, when it looks as though we were forsaken and our ultimate hope betrayed : all these are sufficiently common experiences, and all can be united to the Cross. Here again Christ remains within our limitations. He hallows real life, and invites us to hallow it by the willing consecration of our small humiliations, sacrifices and pains; transmuting them into part of that creative sacrifice, that movement of faith, hope and charity in which the human spirit is most deeply united to the Spirit of God.

And indeed, unless we can do this our world is chaos; for we cannot escape suffering, and we never understand it till we have embraced it, turned it into sacrifice, and given ourselves in it to God. Then, looking from this vantage-point upon the Crucifix, we see beyond the torment and the darkness, the cruel physical pain and its results. As in some of the great creations of mediæval art, we are allowed to discern the peace of a divine and absolute acceptance, a selfless and abandoned love, tranquil, unstrained, strangely full of joy : the joy of suffering accepted and transfigured by the passion of redeeming charity. And in the end, of course, we too only triumph by that which we can endure and renounce. The only victories worth having in any department of life must be won on Calvary.

There is a phrase which the Greek Liturgy constantly applies to God in Christ : " O Lord and Lover of Men ! " The whole meaning and drama of the Passion is gathered up in that. The Evangelists' accounts—all the curt notes crowded together—reveal, when we take them separately and dwell upon them, the deep entrance into human suffering in all its phases, the utter self-giving to the vocation of sacrifice, of One Who is, in completeness, both the Lord and Lover of mankind. Consider some of these episodes. The anointing by the woman of Bethany, of one who never seemed more divine than at this moment, accepting so peacefully the menacing web of events that are closing in ; and then even that gesture of love spoilt by the sordid displeasure of His own disciple. Then the incredible beauty of that two-fold act of selfless generosity, the Last Supper and the Washing of the Feet ; the humble cleansing and feeding of the imperfect human creature, with its deep reverence for that human creature's limitations and concern for that human creature's needs. And then Gethsemane, the real crisis and victory. The first prayer of natural agony : " If it is possible, don't let this happen ! I can't face it." And the second prayer : " If I must go through with this, Thy Will be done." Because of that scene, at the very heart of human suffering, even its rebellions and fears, we are never alone. We often feel that we make a mess of our suffering and lose the essence of sacrifice, waste our opportunity, fail God, because we cannot stand up to it. Gethsemane is the answer of the Divine Compassion to that fear.

After that, He seems to move with a strange serenity through the scenes of the Betrayal and the Trial. If we think of all these events as they actually were, crowded together, beating one after another in swift succession on a soul unique in its sensitiveness to evil, sorrow, and love, and remember that within them went forward the most crucial event in the history of man, we reach a new conviction of the mysterious energy of pain, its necessary presence in all deep religion. We sometimes think we need a " quiet time " before making a great spiritual effort. Our Lord's quiet time was Gethsemane ; and we know what that was like.

At all these points the soul's interior life is moulded very closely on its Pattern. We too, setting our face towards Jerusalem, must serve with humble self-oblivion up to the very end ; meeting every demand on our patience and pity, and faithfully dispensing the Water of Life which may pour through us while leaving our own thirst unquenched. We must, when the moment comes for us, endure in apparent loneliness the assault of sin, agony, and darkness. We too must elect for the Will of God when it means the complete frustration of our own efforts, the apparent death of our very selfhood ; and only so enter into the life-giving life. We cannot expect to reflect the joy and the power of that strange victory, if we dodge the pain and conflict in which it was won. Prayer in darkness and forsakenness, the complete disappearance of everything that could minister to spiritual self-love, humiliating falls and bitter deprivations, the apparent failure even of faith, buffetings of Satan renewed when least expected, long sojourn in that solitary valley where Christian " was so confounded that he did not know his own voice " : these are all part of that long process, which sometimes seems like a plodding journey and sometimes like a swaying battle, through which the mighty purposes of the Divine Charity are fulfilled in human souls.

All this, the Creed assures us, is part of the inner life of man. Little wonder that the Christian must be sturdy about it ; fit for all weathers, and indifferent to his interior ups and downs. Umbrellas, mackintoshes and digestive tabloids are not issued to genuine travellers on this way. Comfort and safety-first must give place to courage and love, if we are to become—as we should be—the travelling agents of the Divine Charity. If the road on which we find ourselves is narrow, with a bad surface and many sudden gradients, it is probably the right route. The obvious and convenient by-pass which skirts the worst hill also by-passes the city set upon the hill : the City of the Contemplation of the Love of God. It gives a very nice general view to the pious motorist ; but those who want to enter the City must put up with the bad approach. After a certain point the right road is marked " unfit for motors," and the traveller must go forward alone.

CHAPTER VI

GLORIFIED

Life is not life if it be not life from death. And God is not God if He be not the end of men.—*Karl Barth.*

When the evening of this life comes, you will be judged on love.—*St. John of the Cross.*

AT the heart of Christianity, the clue to its astonishing history and persistent power, we find a contrast, a crisis, a transformation. The contrast is that between the life before and after Calvary. The crisis which marks the transition is the Passion; that great gesture of unblemished charity in which, as St. John says, " we know love." The transformation is that of man's limited nature, his narrow self, as we know it here, into something new, strange and lovely; possessed of a mysterious power and freedom, a fresh kind of life, and spending this life within our everyday existence to serve and save men. Only a spiritual sequence which is completed in this life-giving life is fully sane and fully Christian. The Pattern which is shown to us is a pattern which lives and moves and changes as we must live and move and change.

Those who give themselves to the life of the spirit are brought bit by bit, as they can bear it and respond to it, to that crisis in which all they have won seems taken away from them; and they are faced by the demand for complete self-surrender, an act of unconditional trust. But this is not the end of the story. The self-abandonment of the Cross is a transition from the half-real to the real ; it is the surrender of our separate self-hood, even our spiritual self-hood—the last and most difficult offering of love— so that we may enter by this strait gate, so hard to find and so unpromising in appearance, that life-giving life of triumphant charity for which humanity is made. Only those who are generous up to the limits of self-loss can hope to become channels of the generosity of God. In that crisis the I, the separate self, with its loves and hates, its personal preoccupations, is sacrificed and left behind. And out of this most true and active death to self, the spirit is reborn into the real life : not in some other trans- cendental world, but in this world, among those who love us and those we love.

So the Crucifix, which is the perfect symbol of generous sacrifice, is the perfect symbol of victory too : of the love which shirks nothing and so achieves everything, the losing and the finding of life. " He was crucified, dead and buried —rose again and ascended." With this double statement the Creed, the rule of prayer, reaches its climax, and shows us in a sentence the deepest meaning of our life : declaring in plain language that unlimited self-offering is the only path from man to God.

This means that the Thought of God, penetrating our tangled world and entering into union with our im- perfect nature, saves and transforms that nature, raises it to a new level, not by power, but by the complete exercise of courageous love ; the deliberate facing of the world's worst. And we, following the footsteps of that holy Life which reveals reality, must take the same way. " As dying and behold we live " is a literal fact for the genuine Chris- tian. The release of power, the transformation of life which comes from unconditional self-abandonment, is guaranteed to us by the story of Easter and the Forty Days : its continuance in the sacraments and the saints. We too achieve all by risking all. Christianity is a triumphant heroism. The valiant obedience of the Blessed Virgin makes the Incarnation possible : the more complete and awful self-giving of the Cross makes the life-giving life of the Church and the Saints possible. The ancient Easter Sequence sums it up :

> Death and Life strove together in awful combat ;
> The Lord of Life, who died, living reigns.

And yet this reign, with its strange triumphant beauty, is not manifested in any of the sensational incidents of which Apocalyptic writers had dreamed ; by a sudden coming in the Clouds of Heaven, or by the shattering of our ordinary human world. Still true to the Divine method of hiddenness and humility, it comes back into that world very quietly ; brought by love, and only recognized by love. It appears by preference in connection with the simple realities of everyday existence, and exercises its enlightening, pacifying, strengthening influence in and through these homely realities. Personal needs, friendly affections, become the consecrated channels of the immortal Love, which declares its victories by a quiet and tender benediction poured out on ordinary life. The glory of the Divine Humanity is not shown in the Temple and the Synagogue. He seeks out His nervous followers within the arena of ordinary life ; meets them behind the locked doors of the Upper Room, waits for them in early morning by the lake side, walks with them on the country road, and suddenly discloses Himself in the breaking of bread. The characters of the old life which are carried through into this new and glorified life are just those which express a homely and cherishing love. It is the One who had fed the multitude, pacified the distracted, washed the dusty feet of His followers and given Himself to be their food, who now re-enters their troubled lives; for their sake, not for His own.

For us, these scenes have an other-worldly beauty. We see them bathed in the supernatural light. But for Peter and Thomas, James and John, they happened under normal conditions of time and place. Frightened, weary and discouraged, worried about the future and remorseful about the past, for them the wonder abode in the quiet return of the Holy and Immortal who was yet the familiar and the human, to the commonplace surroundings in which they had known Him best. Silently disregarding their disappointing qualities, their stupidity, cowardice and lack of trust, He came back to them in a pure impetus of charity; came down to their level as one that serveth, making visible the Invisible Love, and gave the guarantees which their petty standards demanded and their narrow souls could apprehend. Thus, by this unblemished courtesy, "binding His majesty to our lowliness," as the Byzantine liturgy says, He restored their faith, hope and charity; and gave them an example only less searching in its self-oblivious gentleness than the lesson of the washing of the feet.

Even their own fragmentary notes of what happened, or seemed to them to happen, shame and delight us by their witness to the splendour and humility of generous love. "My Lord!" says St. Thomas, seeing, touching, and measuring the Holiness so meekly shown to him in his own crude terms; and then, passing beyond that sacramental revelation to the unseen, untouched, unmeasured, uttering the word every awakened soul longs to utter—" My

God ! " The very heart of the Christian revelation is disclosed in that scene.

So it is that the real mark of spiritual triumph—the possession of that more lovely, more abundant life which we discern in moments of deep prayer—is not an abstraction from this world, but a return to it ; a willing use of its conditions as material for the expression of love. There is nothing high-minded about Christian holiness. It is most at home in the slum, the street, the hospital ward : and the mysteries through which its gifts are distributed are themselves chosen from amongst the most homely realities of life. A little water, some fragments of bread, and a chalice of wine are enough to close the gap between two worlds ; and give soul and senses a trembling contact with the Eternal Charity. By means of these its creatures, that touch still cleanses, and that hand still feeds. The serene, unhurried, self-imparting which began before Gethsemane continues still. Either secretly or sacramentally, every Christian is a link in the chain of perpetual penitents and perpetual communicants through which the rescuing Love reaches out to the world. Perhaps there is no more certain mark of a mature spirituality than the way in which those who possess it are able to enter a troubled situation and say, "Peace," or turn from the exercise of heroic love to meet the humblest needs of men.

One of the few passages of spiritual value in the Apocryphal Gospels, and the only one that has left its mark on the Creed, is that which describes the coming of the soul of Christ into the unseen world of the departed : His " descent into hell " to the rescue of those " spirits in prison " to whom the revelation of the Divine Charity had not been given on earth. Some of the greatest of the mediæval painters have found in that story the perfect image of triumphant love. They show us the liberated soul of Jesus, robed in that humanity which has endured the anguish of the Passion, passing straight from this anguish to the delighted exercise of a saving charity. He comes with an irresistible rush, bearing the banner of redemption to the imprisoned souls of those who knew Him not. There they are, pressing forward to the mouth of the cave ; the darkness, narrowness and unreality from which He comes to free them, at His own great cost. The awed delight of the souls He rescues, is nothing beside the Rescuer's own ecstatic delight. It is as if the charity self-given on Calvary could not wait a moment, but rushed straight to the awaiting joy of releasing the souls of men. There is no hint of the agony and darkness through which He has won the power to do this. Everything is forgotten but the need which the Rescuer is able to meet.

That scene, if we place it—as we should do—before the lovely story of Easter and the Forty Days, helps us to an understanding of their special quality ; and sets before us once for all Rescuing Love as the standard of Christian holiness, and its production in us as the very object of our transformation. For this is our tiny share in that Divine action which brings the supernatural charity right down into the confusions and sorrows of our life, to " save " and transform. Here we look at Sanctity, that " risen life " which has power, and triumphs in virtue of its love. And the deepest truth about ourselves is, that we are human beings ; and therefore have in ourselves the capacity for this same triumph of the power that is love, if we are willing to face the cost. The cost is that crucifying struggle with natural self-love, that passive endurance of the Divine action, which brings the soul out of the narrow, intense, individual life—even though it be apparently a religious life—into the wide self-spending universal life of the Divine Charity. " We know that we have passed out of death into life, because we love the brethren." But tension, suffering, and utter helplessness mark that crucial change.

When Christ said, " My Father and your Father—My God and your God," He made a declaration which must enslave and transfigure the whole lives of those who realize what is implied in it ; conferring on them the tremendous privilege of partnership. " Fellow-workers with God, because co-heirs with Christ." After that, the soul's own life is to be " in the Spirit " : that is, delivered from the tension and struggle of those who are ever striving to adjust the claims of two worlds, because gladly subordinated to the mighty purposes of God. Everything is left behind which does not contribute to those purposes ; and so, all that is left is harmonized within His peace. To them that are perishing, says St. Paul, such a programme is foolishness : " but unto us which are being saved it is the Power of God." It is, in fact, what Christianity really means ; and if Christians chose to stand up to this obligation, they could transform the world.

" Where the Spirit of the Father is," said St. Irenaeus, " there is a Living Man : living because of his share in the Spirit, man because of the substance of his flesh." Other men are, at best, half alive. And the Spirit of the Father is Creative Love. That is the fundamental quality which man shares with God, and which constitutes his kinship with God. Where this rules his life he becomes, in one way or another, an agent of the Eternal Charity. That of course in its perfection is the secret of the Saints ; the cause of what we call their " supernatural power."

" My Father and your Father " means, then, that we are

the children of the Eternal Perfect, Whose essential nature is generous Love ; and that we are destined to manifest the splendour of God in and through the homely scenes, the long and arduous labours, self-givings and sufferings, which the Divine Wisdom irradiated once and irradiates still. It means a new quality of life possible to us and awaiting us ; not somewhere else, but where we are now.

This quality of life is already manifest, wherever the limiting forms of human devotion, human suffering, human service are given in simplicity to the total purposes of God. For Reality has been shown to us incarnate among men, so that we may try to weave its pattern into the texture of human life ; redeeming that life from ugliness, and making it a garment of God. It is not a conspicuous pattern. The shimmer of holiness appears upon the surface mostly in obscure acts of sacrifice and quiet selfless deeds. But when we look behind, and trace this delicate beauty to its source, what we see is a living Love ; so individual, and yet so general, that on one hand the relation of each spirit to that Spirit is unique and complete, and on the other the love poured out on one subtracts nothing from the love given to all.

To realize this is already to move out from the narrow experience of the pious individualist, absorbed in the contemplation of his own spiritual shortcomings and desires, to the glorious liberty of those whose life is cleansed of all self-occupation, and flows out in delighted response to the demand of God and the needs of man : " being made the children of God and of the light," as the baptismal service has it. Our petty worries, faults, anxieties and ignorances, our careful discriminations in practice and belief, even our deplorable rebellions and antipathies fade and shrivel when we see our total destiny like this, and sink our small efforts in the vast tide of the Eternal Spirit's life. We taste then, in our limited way, something of that experience which transfigured the Twelve; imparted to them the life-giving life, and sent them out to spread it through the world.

And indeed, the Christian is required for this and for no other purpose; to be one more worker for the Kingdom, one more transmitter of the Divine Charity, the great spendthrift action of God. From the first, the transmitters have been ordinary faulty people like ourselves. " He gave Himself in either kind," not to a select company of sanctified souls, but to unstable Peter, dubious Thomas, pushful James and John; Paul, who had persecuted Him as sincerely and as savagely as any modern rationalist, and who had consented to His martyr's death. They must have seemed a very unlikely collection. But they were surrendered, and so they could be used; woven into the tissue of that Church which transmits the triumphant and all-sacrificing life.

That life indwells the world and the world knows it not; largely because those to whom it is given fail to disclose it. Christians, that " nation " as the New Testament calls them, who exist only to be the wide-open channels of the inpouring Spirit of Charity, block its passage by their interior hardness, their spiritual selfishness, apathy, love of comfort, their petty and sterile religious outlook. They are too timid, too ca' canny, to risk losing their own lives; to give themselves with undemanding generosity, in order to find the all-generous Life of God.

It is easy enough to appreciate the lovely vision of that all-generous Life, poured out through human channels to transform the life of men. All our religious pussy cats can enjoy the beauty of the design, and bask in the golden light which illuminates it. Their vague idealism and fussy optimism and sentimental other-worldliness all feel warmer and brighter when that radiance falls upon them. But they do not care to face the fact that the design is a working-drawing, which we are required to carry out with the homely materials in hand. The worth of men is not judged by their admiration of its beauty, but by the perfection with which it is reproduced within their own lives. That which we are shown in contemplation we are required to express in action : not by our peculiar beliefs and punctual religious practices, but simply by the exercise of Rescuing Love.

The immortal Figure of Christ, God's pattern for humanity, stands over against life ; and judges it by irradiating it. He sets the standard, shows what man is meant to be ; revealing Himself in every demand on our generosity, however homely, and by that demand alone and our response to it separating the real from the unreal, the living from the dead. Yet in the deepest sense, even that response is not truly our own. It is the One God, indwelling in His deep humanity His little human creatures, Who stirs in us and initiates each movement of Charity ; " secretly inciting," says von Hügel, " what He openly crowns."

And now we begin to see a certain sequence in those mysteries through which His Reality is brought into focus for us ; or, in the language of theology, " the Word is made flesh." That sequence begins where life begins right down in the natural order, leaving no phase of our common experience outside the radiance of love. It develops among homely things, quietly, slowly, and without sensational incidents ; subject to all the common tests, strains, joys and duties of our human existence, and through and within them increasing in wisdom and stature. Confronted in the deep solitude of the wilderness by man's crucial choice between self-interest and self-loss, this Life rejects everything that is less than God ; everything that ministers to self-will. So, emerging into the unsullied light of truth it manifests truth ; teaching the Will of God for men, and the path men must follow to God. And because this is the life of One who sees men as they are, knowing what is in man, there pours out through it that wide, loving and creative compassion which is the only source of healing and of help. By the interplay of that pure truth and that warm compassion, it becomes filled with a rescuing and redeeming Power, which transcends difficulties and does not notice dangers ; and this Power is made perfect in sacrifice—the Eucharist, Gethsemane, and the Cross. Thus by a path which never departs from the human landscape we are led out and up beyond the human landscape, to a Divine revelation that yet is deeply human, and a human revelation that is completely Divine.

PART III

CHAPTER VII

SPIRIT

The Holy Spirit is God as He is everywhere and at all times.—
St. Thomas Aquinas.

God is no otherwise your God than as he is the God of your life,
manifested in it; and he can be no otherwise the God of your
life but as his Spirit is living within you.—*William Law.*

IF the first part of the Creed took our minds right away
from our personal struggles and experiences, and
brought into focus the great Fact of God, and the second
part showed us the self-revelation in history of that Absolute Love, setting the standard of reality for men; the
third part turns our attention back to the conditions under
which we are to live out our own lives. It describes the
position in which the action of the Eternal Charity in history has placed us; our here-and-now experience of an
all-penetrating Divine Spirit, the supernatural energy we
are given, the supernatural organism of which we form
part, the supernatural achievement towards which we
move.

All this opens up for us a wholly new vista of what
Henry Martyn used to call " the mysterious glories of
religion." We have been shown the sky of stars, enchant-
ing and overwhelming us: and now we realize that we
are living the star-life too. One of these shining worlds,
held within Eternity and kept by the Eternal Charity, is
our own. " I am not a God afar off. I am thy Maker and

Friend." We think now of that One God's intimate presence with us and support of us ; as a living, acting, holy Spirit penetrating the whole world and each soul in that world. We recognize His ceaseless pressure on and in our spirits, His generous and secret self-giving on which we depend so entirely : the way in which we, with our limited spiritual powers, experience His energetic love, and the way we are required to respond to it.

" I believe in the Holy Spirit, the Lord, and Giver of Life." All kinds of life ; nothing is specified. That mysterious thing Life, then, is declared to be given and sustained by the generous Spirit of Charity ; poured out from the fresh springs of that fontal Being we call Father, and that loving Wisdom, that Creative Thought, we call Son. In its essence it is holy ; we are merely the more or less adequate forms that it vivifies and upholds. To say, " I believe that the Eternal Godhead, whose unspeakable majesty I adore, pours out His holy and living Spirit on and in all flesh " means that we recognize with awe a close and mysterious union between God and all things He has made : the Artist-Lover present and active in all that creation which He loves. And in human beings this close union and constant life-giving action is especially to be recognized and declared, with gratitude and awe. We believe, then, that the Living God is the direct cause and source of all our living : and not this alone, but of all the lives we touch, all by whom we are attracted and by whom we are repelled. We believe that there is no place or cranny where He is not ; no situation in which He is not interested and in which He does not act—none, therefore, to which we can refuse interest, or in which we can dare to do less than our best. When our inward and outward action literally and actually correspond with this august belief—but not before—we shall be living the Life of Faith.

If we put some of the things which the New Testament says about this aspect of religion, alongside the declarations of the Creed, we receive a tremendous impression of the actuality of this experience of a penetrating and life-giving Spirit, the Divine Generosity acting as a distinct and personal energy within the human scene. " We have all been made to drink of one Spirit," says St. Paul, as if this ineffable truth were a commonplace of Christian experience. And this Spirit, says the Creed, is both Lord and Life-giver; the Absolute God acting, and bringing the whole Trinity into the soul, which thus becomes the temple of the Holy Giver of Life. To enter that sanctuary, shut the door, and there find Him, is a very important part of the life of prayer.

Yet only a part; for this inward communion cannot remain steady and unblemished for very long. Something, the jar of circumstance, or the deeper disharmony of our own nature, breaks in to spoil it. Then we need the completing experience; when we recognize our own insufficiency, and our weakness and dimness must be made good by a fresh gift out of the riches of the Divine Charity, ever holding in reserve for us more than we have guessed or known. When we seem to open our door and expose our emptiness, and a strange power pours in to enhance and enlighten; and we go out strong in that power, but not in ourselves. " In that hour," says Christ, " do what the Spirit shall say unto you." " It is the Spirit," says St. Paul, " who maketh intercession for us." " The Spirit *fell* on them," says the writer of *Acts*. If we look at all this, and consider that it describes our real situation as Christian souls—little spirits supported by the infinite Spirit of Divine Love—we surely receive a new vision of

G

the richness of our inheritance, and the greatness of our responsibility.

In the Fourth Gospel, the strange word " Paraclete " enters the Christian vocabulary as the best available term for this experience of the Spirit of God acting within our lives. Our nearest meaning for " Paraclete " seems to be, " One who is called to stand alongside us," or stands by us to give us support. So we are given the marvellous vision of the infinite Divine Charity, Giver of all life, ever standing alongside our small derived spirits in their efforts and struggles. " Hold Thou up my goings in Thy path that my footsteps slip not." In that most intimate and practical of all prayers, the small unsteady spirit of man acknowledges its real situation ; even though we often have the illusion of fighting it out alone, for the Charity which keeps life never coddles it. The maturing of our personality, its full transformation in God, could hardly be achieved unless we were left in an apparent independence ; to suffer, accept, deal with circumstances as real incarnate spirits, subject to all the vicissitudes of physical life. Our courage and loyalty must be tested by a genuine experience of solitude and darkness, if all our latent possibilities are to be realized.

"O Lord, your battles *do* last a long time ! " said poor Suso, worn out by the disciplines, sufferings and reverses through which his ardent but unsteady soul was brought into stability and peace. Certainly life is not made soft for Christians, though it is in the last resort made safe. Nor do the struggles of the spiritual life—even the most crucial and most heroic—either look or feel very glorious while they are going on. Muddy trenches, great watchfulness and weariness, a limited view, endless small duties and deprivations, and no certainty as to whether we are winning or not ; these are the conditions of the long struggle for the victory of disinterested love. It is often the patient defence of an unnoticed corner which decides the result. The difference between the real spiritual experiences even of sanctity, and the popular notion of them, is the difference between the real private in the trenches, and the glossy photograph of the same warrior, taken when he is at home on leave.

Yet the whole power and life of the Invisible God, the Divine Charity itself, stands by us in the trenches. " As ye are partakers of the suffering, so are ye of the support," says St. Paul to the Corinthians. The two things go together. The Spirit of Life stands alongside all those who are really living, making a genuine effort to stand up to the heroic obligations of the soul ; not by those who value religion for its consolations, and treat their faith as a feather-bed. The energy of love will never do for us that which we ought to do for ourselves ; but will ever back up the creature's efforts by its grace, coming into action just where our action fails. This is a secret that has always been known to men and women of prayer ; something we can trust, and that acts in proportion to our trust. Sometimes it is on our soul that the tranquillizing touch is laid : sometimes the hurly-burly of our emotional life, which threatens to overwhelm us, is mysteriously stilled. Sometimes events, which we think must destroy us or those whom we love, are strangely modified by the Spirit that indwells and rules them. More and more as we go on with the Christian life we learn the absolute power of Spirit over circumstance : seldom sensationally declared, but always present and active. God in His richness and freedom coming as a factor into every situation ; over-ruling the stream of events which make up our earthly existence, and through these events moulding our souls, quickening and modifying our lives at every point.

This general free action of the Power of God within life is what we rather vaguely call Providence. Its pressure and activity is of course continuous in and through the whole texture of that life, though usually unperceived by us. But now and then it emerges on the surface to startle us by its witness to a subtle and ceaseless will and love working within the web of events; and we perceive that the enfolding mystery has the character of Living Mind. I am sure that we ought to reckon with this mysterious fact far more than we usually do. Evidence of the free and direct action of God lies very thick on the pages of the New Testament. It has always been the decisive factor in the lives of the Saints; manifested the more clearly in proportion to their simplicity, surrender and confidence of soul. How marvellously those lives develop—Augustine, Francis, Catherine, Teresa, Vincent de Paul, the Curé d'Ars—once they have given themselves into the Hand of God. Sometimes a strange power seems to control great events in their interest; sometimes it moulds by small touches a homely career to the greater purposes of love. " The power of God present unto salvation," says St. Paul (not the power of God present unto comfort); this is the very essence of the Gospel. We are held and penetrated by a personal Spirit, a never-ceasing Presence, that intervenes to use or over-rule events. The more freely, simply and humbly the soul is abandoned to this penetrating and encompassing power, the more it becomes conscious— dimly and yet surely—of its constant, stern, yet loving, action through all the circumstances of life. To resist that action means conflict and suffering. To accept it may still mean suffering; but a suffering that is sweetened by love.

The German mystics used to speak of the spiritual life as the School of the Holy Spirit. There was an upper school and a lower school. In the upper school only one thing was taught : the science of perfect self-abandonment —that death to self which is the condition of all full and vigorous life. The lessons given in the upper school were hard and painful ; but the teacher was the Divine Charity. Darkness, loneliness, the apparent loss of God, unexpected humiliations, mortifying struggles with our own temperaments, all enter into the curriculum of the upper school. In the lower forms 'the educational method is gentler and more pleasant. But when we face the really tough lessons of the interior course, it is like the first time that we are introduced to algebra or metaphysics. We are suddenly made aware of unrealized worlds, and are completely baffled, conscious only of our own utter ignorance and helplessness. Instead of the neat exercise books, the tidy meditations, the orderly self-examinations and prayers to which we have been accustomed, we are left floundering. The Teacher now uses the direct method, and we have to find out how best to respond. No use to rely on those excellent manuals which offered to teach us " how to make our approach to God." Here God makes His approach to the soul. He comes and invades our life in strange disguises, and purifies us in ways that we cannot recognize. The first thing we are taught is our own ignorance and nothingness, our total dependence on the Spirit of Life ; and our whole inner life is simplified by this, and becomes a humble, mere self-opening to that Spirit who is the real doer of all that we do and the teacher of all that we know. " Lord, my spirit faileth. Hide not thy face from me. Cause me to hear thy loving kindness in the morning, for in thee do I trust. Cause me to know the

way in which I should walk for I lift up my soul unto thee
. . . teach me to do thy will, for thou art my God. Thy
Spirit is good. . . . Quicken me, O Lord, I am thy servant." In the upper school we learn the entire and direct
dependence which turns this prayer into a perpetual and
natural conversation between our small spirits and the
Spirit of God.

" Let yourself be guided by My rules," said the voice of
that Spirit to Pascal. " See how well I have led the Blessed
Virgin and the Saints, who have let Me act through them."
There one of the most acute and subtle intellects which
humanity has produced, enters the upper school and list-
ens to the one lesson it teaches. " Let Me act "—not resisting, setting up conflicts, capitulating to cowardice or
disguised self-interest, but docile to the quiet movements
and pressure of the Divine Charity however strange and
unexpected they may be. Those courageous spirits who
have done this have always been justified of their trust.
They have accepted the only possible position of the human
will and thus become the tools and instruments of the
Universal Will, the Lord and Giver of Life, by whom
alone all that is worth doing is done. " Behold the handmaid of the Lord ! "—this is humanity's total contribution
to the mystery of Holiness, because this alone can
open the door to the transforming supernatural energy.
Saints are simply persons who are sufficiently self-abandoned to let the Spirit act through them ; instead of per-
sisting in self-chosen and self-interested activities.

Thus it seems idiotic as well as unworthy to refuse those
acts of self-opening and self-abandonment which make the
human soul accessible to that boundless life : cowardly
and stupid to fail in responding to the training that is always being given to us through circumstance, and by mak-

ing us more sensitive to the pressure of God educates us for that particular position in the scheme for which we were made. " Progress in the interior life," " spiritual power," and other great things of which we speak with an easy admiration, sometimes complaining that they do not seem to come our way, can only come by this way: by a humble, persevering and courageous conformity to the Lord and Giver of Life, an ever deepening surrender to the total movement of the Spirit's will, an ever more peaceful acceptance of His gradual transforming action on us, supported in the difficult process of change by the " grace of His Unchangeableness."

Christ seems to have thought of prayer as, above all, a way in which our little spirits may become more and more accessible to the life of that Eternal Spirit. His teaching about prayer hinges on our human poverty and need as towards the Holy Spirit; and that boundless Life and Love pressing in on us, responding to every demand, search and supplication, making good our needs, because it is Love. Everyone that asks receives, and he that seeks finds, the Holy Spirit. The one thing He considers worth asking for, the true object of prayer, is this concrete gift of the Spirit of God, for which alone we hunger, seek, and clamour at the frontiers of the unseen world. The Spirit which creates, penetrates and keeps us, feeds and illuminates us, enters our lives and presses through them to other lives, has far more in reserve for us than we have yet received; and our real growth is a growth in longing for that total and transfiguring presence. But the Spirit is one of those guests for whom space must be made; whose presence makes a difference to the whole house, and not merely to the spare room. We give the invitation at our own risk, not knowing which of our old easy-going ways will be incompatible with this Presence; which enters as Lord, as well as giver of life, making demands and setting going activities which must take precedence of everything else. For we are really asking that the life and energy of the Absolute God shall enter and use our premises, and recondition them to suit the purposes of Charity: and this means more than fresh curtains and a little whitewash.

The ordained end of the whole interior of life is the unconditional giving of this invitation, which brings an unconditional response: replacing our ignorant and restless action by the boundless living action, the energetic Spirit of the one God. The Liturgy, which is the voice of the praying Church, declares this again and again; as we should realize if we would listen, and take its words literally, as they are meant. " Mercifully grant that thy Holy Spirit may in all things direct and rule our hearts." " That we may daily increase in thy Holy Spirit more and more." " Cleanse the thoughts of our hearts by the inspiration of thy Holy Spirit." " That we may be renewed day by day by thy Holy Spirit." There is something definite and practical about all this. It is an appeal from the limited to the Limitless, in Whom we live and move ; to the personal action of the Godhead, both transcending and indwelling His creation as " maker, lover and keeper " of all that is made.

So too self-giving to the purposes of Spirit, entering that mighty current of living Charity, means entering into a real communion with other souls, who are linked to us within that tide ; and is the secret of that strange power which is exercised by men and women of prayer. When General Gordon was at Darfur, working for the suppression of the slave trade, that great man of action wrote this in his diary :

" Praying for the people whom I am about to visit gives me much strength; and it is wonderful how something seems already to have passed between us, when I meet with a chief (for whom I have prayed) for the first time."

Such a statement as that brings with it a sense of all our small human affairs as bathed in, embraced by Eternal Spirit; and of our dullness and blindness in not making this truth the ruling fact of our lives. If something has passed within the world of Spirit between two persons who are about to have a difficult interview or whose sympathy is incomplete—if one has sought the other in that ocean of the Divine Charity which bathes both their souls—the meeting may still call for mutual patience, may mortify self-will or self-love; but all will now take place within the Universal Spirit, which cherishes the true interests of both, and is the bond between them. So, the carrying forward of all our human relationships into the stream of the Creative Love, means making the interests of others —already deeply interesting to God—our interests too; and is the essence of real intercession, which, like all creative prayer, requires as its preliminary death to self and life to Him.

And last, the Holy Spirit in whom the Christian believes is not only a boundless source of life and of support, but One who is declared to " speak by the prophets." A prophet is an individual seized and used as the organ of the Voice of God; a channel, along which news of Eternity reaches the human world. We think of the prophet as a great figure charged with a mysterious message; but the early Church did not limit the word like this. As the experience of Spirit was a recognized fact, so the prophet too was a recognized type in Christian society. He was the person subordinated to God, chosen and used by God;

and therefore possessed of a certain initiative and freedom. He constantly corrected the tendency of institutional religion to be the slave of its own routine ; tempering the churchy mood by the disconcerting freshness of the supernatural world, the clear, awestruck vision and stern demands of a disinterested love.

The prophet continues, under many names, to be one of the channels through which the Creative Spirit acts within the human world : teaching and directing men through men. Thus all spiritual literature has a prophetic character. Like poetry, it is greater than the mind that produces it ; and is charged with a message from the supernatural world for which this mind is merely the channel and instrument. We cannot set any limit to the work which feeble, sinful and apparently unsuitable individuals can do for God, when they are called and used by the Spirit. " I formed thee, I knew thee, I sanctified thee," says the Voice to the reluctant and astonished Jeremiah : " I have appointed thee a prophet unto the nations." Jeremiah's terrified response, " Ah, Lord God ! I cannot speak, for I am a child ! " is entirely beside the point. The initiative does not lie with the vessel so unexpectedly chosen, but with the Divine Life pouring in and through it. " Whatsoever I shall command thee, thou shalt speak . . . be not afraid. I am with thee to deliver thee saith the Lord." Jeremiah, sensitive to spiritual reality, and therefore to his own utter inadequacy, and the real awfulness of that which he is called to do, is by that very fact made fit to be a channel of God : for only those who recognize their own inadequacy even begin to be adequate to the Spirit's demands. He speaks by the prophets, surrendered and self-emptied : does not tell the prophets to express their own admirable ideas.

In his own small way the ordinary Christian must be prepared for all this ; because it is a part of the economy of that spiritual world in which we live. He must expect to hear the Voice of the Spirit speaking through very unexpected and unsuitable messengers, and even perhaps to be seized and used in his own turn for some bit of work which will further the purposes of the Charity of God. That living Charity in its freedom and power acts most often in defiance of our limitations, prejudices and expectations ; does not necessarily engage its servants at the best registry office, or take those with a good character from their last place. The story of the sudden call of the diffident and timid Jeremiah is read by the Church on the Feast of the Conversion of St. Paul ; pressing on us the sense of the priority of the living God, His personal action, His disconcerting freedom, coming to us in history, speaking by the mouths of very peculiar people, chosen according to His view not ours and accomplishing His purposes sometimes by wandering roads and sometimes by straight. " You are a chosen vessel to Me," says the Voice to the astonished persecutor of the Church : " You happen to be the right shape for My purpose ; and that is the only thing that matters. The sudden blazing impact of truth, the agony of shame, the tremendous discipline to which I call you, will complete your preparation for the work I shall give you to do, the place in the scheme which you alone can fill." For there is no creature, however rebellious and however imperfect, who cannot be transformed to the purposes of the Spirit of God ; ruling His Creation from within as Lord and Life-giver, and secretly and subtly determining the path of every soul.

CHAPTER VIII

CHURCH

Ye are fellow-citizens with the saints and of the household of God . . . builded together for a habitation of God in the Spirit.— *St. Paul.*

Souls—all human souls—are deeply interconnected . . . the Church at its best and deepest is just that—that interdependence of all the broken and the meek, all the self-oblivion, all the reaching-out to God and souls.—*F. von Hügel.*

THE old Flemish painters loved to represent the Church as a vast cathedral, with many side chapels opening from one great nave. In the centre of that nave stood the Crucifix. In the surrounding chapels those Sacraments were dispensed through which the Incarnate Charity pours itself out to purify, feed, restore, and at last transform the feeble lives of men ; dependent on that ceaseless self-giving, as branches upon the Vine. That was a wonderful image of what Christianity really is; the manifestation in and through men of the self-spending Charity of God, and the binding together in one Divine Society of all who have been touched by that supernatural generosity and depend on its life-giving life.

Thinking of this, we are no longer surprised that the Creed which once ended by stating its belief in the Spirit, should go on to insist on belief in the Body, the Temple, that Spirit indwells ; asserting the social and organic character of real spirituality, endorsing its authority and repudiating the claims of the religious individualist. " I believe One Catholic and Apostolic Church." We must believe someone. We believe, then, the united voice of Christendom ; its statements about Reality, as given in its Scriptures, its Liturgy, its Sacraments, and by its Saints. We make its Creeds, its solemn pronouncements regarding the essentials of Faith, our standard, trust them, take them seriously : not as a particular way of dealing with life— something that happens to appeal to us—but as *the* way of dealing with life. Though the architecture be old-fashioned and the lighting defective, here God in His humility tabernacles among men.

So, because we believe in that holy and life-giving Spirit who becomes articulate in the prophets, telling us their vision of God, we also believe, which is often far more difficult, the voice of the traditional Church. When that voice has a horribly official accent, or makes to our minds impossibly concrete statements, we acknowledge that it is possibly our stupidity and not her stuffiness which makes our sympathy so incomplete. She does offer to us —and not to us alone, but to everyone who will listen— the supernatural poetry and the supernatural music on a wave-length we can receive. She witnesses within the world to the Fact of God. All her symbolic veils do give us something of the radiance of the uncreated Light, and within her ancient phrases we hear the murmur of the one Word. And more than this, we acknowledge that the total Christian society, the " Company of Faithful People "—even as we experience it here, in the unfortunate form of a club which is far too full of mutually exclusive *cliques*—has yet a quality, a personality, a power of its own. Its baptism, the mutual act in which we enter its ranks and it cleanses and receives us, does something ; knocks off the fetters of our sub-human past, admits us to a new level of life, makes us the citizens of another Patria, with a real and awful series of privileges and powers and a real and awful series of responsibilities.

All this seems terribly concrete to the enthusiast for " pure spirituality " : and when we think of pews and hassocks and the Parish Magazine, we tend to rebel against the yoke of official religion, with its suggestion of formalism and even frowstiness. It seems far too stiff and institutional, too unventilated, to represent the generous and life-giving dealings of the Divine Charity with men. The chorus which exclaimed with awe and delight, " I believe in one God ! " thins out a good deal when it comes to saying, " I believe in one Church ! " The first lifted us to heaven ; the second brings us down on to the cocoanut matting with a run. Yet there it is ; the Christian sequence is God-Christ-Spirit-Church-Eternal Life. No link in this chain can be knocked out, without breaking the current of love which passes from God through His creatures back again to God. The incarnation of the Holy in this world is social. We are each to contribute our bit to it, and each to depend on the whole. It is not the ardent individual devotee, the supposed recipient of special graces, ruled by special lights and experiences, who is the Bride of Christ. The whole Body is the Bride of Christ : a Body, as St. Paul says, having many different members, some of a very odd shape, some of a very lowly kind. And it is in this Body, at once mysterious and homely, that the individual Christian must consent to sink his life, in order that he may find true life.

Because of this deep fact of the Living Church, this interconnection of all surrendered spirits, the prayer of one unit can avail for all. We pray as an organism, not as a mere crowd of souls ; like grains of rice that happen to

be part of the same pudding. " I believe in the Holy
Catholic Church, the Communion of Saints," says the
Apostles' Creed, putting the same truth in a different way.
Here that rich New Testament word " Communion "
bears a double reference. For on one hand it means that
we believe in the whole fellowship, the society of saints,
known and unknown, living and dead, their reality and
power, their aliveness, their authority, their witness to the
facts of the spiritual life ; and on the other hand that we
believe there is a true communion, a genuine sharing between all the members of the one Body. Within its universal prayer thinker and lover, sufferer and worker,
Catholic and Quaker, pool their resources. When we are
confounded by sudden visions of a holiness and self-
abandonment beyond our span, our share in the Communion of Saints assures us that other souls will suffer and
adore for us, and make up for our deficiencies by their
more abundant life. For since the life of the saints is the
life of charity, they cannot keep anything for themselves
alone. The Life by which they live is shared, commun-
icated from one to another, as the sap of the Vine is given
through the greater branches to the less.

When the Christian looks at the Crucifix, he looks at
that which is for him the Pattern of all perfection ; the
double revelation of God's love towards man and man's
love towards God, the heart of Charity. But he is also·
looking at the Church, that real Church which is a holy
and living Sacrifice eternally self-offered to God ; the
Body of Christ, the number of whose members no man
knows but God alone, and which is the living instrument
of His creative love within this world. " Wherever Christ
is," said St. Ignatius of Antioch, " there is the Catholic
Church." So, to be a member of the Church means not

merely conformity to an institution, but incorporation in
that living organism which only exists to express the
Thought of God. It means becoming part of that perpetual sacrifice which continues in space and time the life
of Incarnate Charity. In the name of all her members,
the Church comes up to the altar with awe and thanks-
giving, and there, on the very frontiers of the unseen
world, she gives herself that she may receive the Food of
Eternal Life. So the inner life of each one of those members must have in it the colour of sacrifice, the energy of
a redeeming love, if it is to form part of the living Soul
of the Church. The unceasing liturgic life of the official
Church, her prayer and adoration, her oblation and communion, only has meaning as the expression of that soul :
the voice of the Communion of Saints. But as this, it has
a meaning, a splendour and a claim on us, far transcending
those private prayers to which we are apt to give priority.
The whole poetry of man's relation to the unseen Love is
hidden in the Liturgy : with its roots in history, its eyes
set upon Eternity, its mingled outbursts of praise and
supplication, penitence and delight, it encloses and carries
forward the devotion of the individual soul, lost in that
mighty melody. To say, then, that we believe the corporate voice of those who make this melody, whose
separate lives are lost in it and who are our companions in
the Way, begins to look like common sense. We are
units in their mighty procession ; and they can teach us
how to walk.

If, then, we thus believe in the Church as a living
spiritual reality, we must act in harmony with that belief,
as members of the Church. This means much more than
doing our bit in the matter of corporate worship ; though
it will certainly include that expression of our social

obligations. It will mean, says St. Paul, " becoming obedient from the heart "—the very core of personality— " to that form of teaching whereunto ye were delivered." That is a demand for the complete transformation of life. It means that being Members of the Body of Christ is to be the ruling fact about us. Crossing over to the divine side with all our powers, we must take a humble place in the ranks : become part of the reasonable, holy and living sacrifice. It means that in work and prayer, suffering and self-conquest, we are never to forget that we do not act alone or for ourselves. We act with and for the whole body. The prayer of the individual Christian is always the prayer of the whole Church ; and therefore it is infinite in its scope.

In his letter to the Romans, we find St. Paul asking his converts if they realize what it means to be part of the Church. It means, he says (and we can imagine their surprise when they heard it), being received into the death of Christ—the unconditional sacrifice of the Cross—in order to walk in newness of life : transformed through self-loss into a bit of that Body which is indwelt and ruled by the Spirit of Divine Charity. No easy application for membership, then, fulfils the demands of real Christianity. It is a crisis, a radical choice, a deep and costly change. When we judge our own lives by this standard we realize that full entrance into the Church's real life must for most of us be a matter of growth. There are layers of our minds, both personal and corporate, still untransformed ; not indwelt by Charity, resisting the action of God. There are many things the Spirit could do through us, for the healing and redeeming of the world, if it were not for our cowardice, slackness, fastidiousness, or self-centred concentration on our own jobs. The individual Christian

H

cannot attain his full stature till he throws in his hand with the saints and the angels : more, with the broken, the struggling and the meek. But most of us are too prudent, too careful to do that. It will not be to us that the great Angel of the Apocalypse, emptied of self-interest and ready for all jobs, will say as he said to St. John, " I am your fellow-slave."

" Present yourselves to God as alive from the dead," says St. Paul ; and your members—all you have, every bit of you—as instruments, tools, of righteousness. That is his standard of churchmanship. That is the kind of life into which he conceives his converts are baptized ; and there is something desperately vigorous and definite about it. What he seems to envisage in the Church is a vast distributing system of the Divine Charity. As we were slaves of " sin "—that is, held tight in a life which is alien from the real purposes of God, off the track, and uses its great energies for its own ends—so, that taking of a new direction which is involved in becoming a Christian, means the turning over of all that energy to God's purposes ; using it for Him, co-operating with the Spirit working within life for the redemption and hallowing of the whole world. That is what the Church is for ; and the Sacraments are there to help those who are prepared to pull their weight.

If, then, we are sufficiently self-emptied and courageous, that Spirit who *is* the Church will act on the world through us. We have accepted a situation which is infinite in its possibilities. The Power that desires to fill and use us, is the Power that filled and used Paul and Augustine, Benedict, Bruno and Bernard, Francis of Assisi and Catherine of Siena, Fox and Wesley ; that went to the ends of the earth with Francis Xavier and Henry Martyn, or trans-

formed a narrow sphere in Father Wainright and the
Curé d'Ars. All alike are " God-bearers, Christ-bearers,
bearers of holy things." The Spirit of Christ is the Church,
and the standard of courage, love and self-oblivion the
Church asks from each of its members is His standard. Until
she gets it her true work cannot be done. We are " called
to be Saints "—self-emptied vessels of the Holy—not for
our own sake but for the sake of the world. Every Christian has to look squarely at this ideal. It does not merely
mean self-loss in an organized religious society, which
depends on God and believes in Him, and teaches morals
and faith. It means self-loss in the world's workshop,
" tools of righteousness unto God "; every ounce of
energy, all powers and talents, initiative, skill and taste,
used—not for us, but for Him. When we contrast this
programme with man's average outlook, it is obvious that
real entrance into the Living Church may well be described
as a death. For some it is a very peaceful death ; but for
some a desperate struggle. " You are *buried* in baptism,"
says St. Paul to his converts. There is something terrible,
a genuine crisis demanding real courage and trust, involved in choosing God.

In the ancient mysteries the cave of initiation was very
dark and forbidding, and the neophyte had to face that as
his first test. So in the soul's secret experience, that pur-
ification of which Baptism is the outward symbol, and
which admits us to the deep life of the Soul of the Church,
must often seem a death to the easy-going agreeable ways
of natural religion. For then we enter the full communion
of a Body whose rhythm of life reproduces that of its Master.
That which was done at the Annunciation remains the type
of the continued action of the Spirit on the Church ; an
action which demands the unconditional self-giving and

humble courage of every Christian soul, that so the Mystical Body may continue in space and time the Incarnation and its awful work.

As, then, we believe in the Holy Spirit—Divine Love, issuing eternally from the Heart of God—we believe also in the Church, the Divine Society, the matrix which receives and gives expression to that love ; and we acknowledge that by entering this Society our whole situation is changed. We become by this act part of a Body, a Communion, in which the Spirit is perpetually re-born in poverty and hardness ; and perpetually continues in and through its Saints—here in one way, there in another—its ceaseless oblation of love. A body in which every living cell is, as St. John Eudes boldly insisted, " part of Christ Himself " ; part of the redeeming life at work within the world. Part, therefore, of a life which may be called to endure betrayal, mockery, crucifixion, darkness and apparent defeat, and give new life through this apparent defeat.

This means that the sufferings of the Body, all its divisions, struggles, persecutions, imperfections, deeply concern every member, and that the mysterious sacrificial action of the Body, which embraces, sweetens and sanctifies all its activities and turns them into love, must also be the secret action of each soul. For the Eucharist is the characteristic act towards God and towards men of the whole Church : a great movement of adoring gratitude, an offering to Him of natural and to them of supernatural gifts, a deep participation in the self-given life of the Divine Charity. And in the Eucharist the principal and invisible actor, " Priest and Victim " in the ancient language of the Liturgy, is Christ, whose members we are. Thus in the Prayer of Humble Access we are really asking for full participation in the life of the Church, with all the mysterious privileges and the solemn obligations of those who are, as St. Ambrose says, " made partakers of the Supreme Divinity."

It is true that such a vocation in its wholeness is far too much for most of us. It can only be a corporate undertaking. Not all can contemplate the Eternal Realities, or enter into the awful mystery of the Cross. But all—including the large and endearing class of spiritual tweenies, ever ready to help with any job—have some place and task within that economy : that triumph of balanced energy and eternal peace. We must be ready for whatever bit falls to our own share—probably not the bit that we expected or desired—and in our secret life towards God, must be so humble, supple, and self-giving, so austere in our demands, that we are kept in training for the test, and wide open to that Spirit who is both the transformer and the ruler of those to whom He comes in power. This lays a great responsibility on every Christian; for it means that our self-discipline, our prayer, our renunciations, our struggles, are not undertaken merely for our own sakes. They are required of us, in order that we may be made more fit for this great vocation, and so increase the energy of the Church. The shallow notion of the life of prayer as a form of spiritual selfishness wilts before this vision of the destiny of the awakened soul.

In the world of spirit, that which is done by one is done for all, since the real actor is always the Charity of God. A Christian's inner life, however deeply hidden, is never private. So far as it is real, the Spirit who indwells the Church prays and adores in him, strives in him and reaches out through him. Therefore, because of the Church, when we pray we pray with all the Saints : in whom this is happening too. Thus the radiation of the humblest prayer affects the whole Body's life, and when we fail to do our part its whole spiritual effectiveness is correspondingly diminished. Our penance is an earnest of its contrite love, our communions add to its total vitality. We go into training in Lent, not as solitary perfectionists interested in our own progress, but as loyal members of a team. We cultivate our soul's little garden not as an allotment, but as part of the great garden of God; and therefore do not expect it to grow every kind of flower and vegetable at once. We are added to the Church, as Cardinal Mercier said, not merely for the sake of our own souls, but " in order to extend the Kingdom of Love."

For the reality of the Church does not abide in us ; it is not a spiritual Rotary Club. Its reality abides in the One God, the ever-living One whose triune Spirit fills it by filling each one of its members. We build up the Church best, not by a mere overhaul of the fabric and the furniture, desirable as this may sometimes be, but by opening ourselves more and more with an entire and humble generosity to that Spirit-God Who is among us as one that serveth, and reaches out through His Church towards the souls of men. Thus the real life of that Church consists in the mutual love and dependence, the common prayer, adoration and self-offering of the whole inter-penetrating family of spirits who have dared to open their souls without condition to that all-demanding and all-giving Spirit of Charity, in Whom we live and move and without Whom we should not exist.

CHAPTER IX

THE WORLD TO COME

I will ask of God such an enlargement of soul, that I may love him with ardour, serve him with joy, and transmit his radiance to the world.—*Elizabeth Leseur.*

And after long woe suddenly our eyes shall be opened; and in clearness of light our sight shall be full.—*Julian of Norwich.*

THE Christian account of the nature of Reality ends with a declaration of absolute confidence. " I look for the resurrection of the dead, and the life of the world to come:" or, more literally, " I expect the life of the age that is drawing near." I expect Eternity as the very meaning and goal of all full human life, and especially of the Christian art of living. I expect it because I have already experienced it; if not in my own person, then by my share in the experience of the Saints. " Let us press on to perfection," says the writer of the Epistle to the Hebrews, " because we have *tasted* of the heavenly gift and the powers of the world to come." The closing phrases of the Creed call us to ascend in heart and mind to the world of the Eternal Perfect, the Thought of God, the Country of Everlasting Clearness, and find the meaning of existence there.

It is as if the soul said, " I believe in and utterly trust one living Perfect God, and His creative purpose, His ceaseless action. And because of that—because I have glimpsed the sparkle of His mysterious radiance and heard the whisper of His inexorable demands—I trust and go on trusting, in spite of all disconcerting appearances, my best and deepest longings. I expect the fulfilment of that sacramental promise which is present in all beauty : the perfect life of the age, the world, that keeps on drawing near. I look past process and change, with all their difficulties and obscurities, to that Perfection which haunts me ; because I know that God is perfect, and His supernatural purpose must prevail."

So, since the Christian life of prayer looks through and beyond Time towards Eternity, finds its fulfilment in Eternity, and ever seeks to bring Eternity into Time, the note that we end on is and must be the note of inexhaustible possibility and hope. Because we believe in the Eternal God, whose very nature is creative Charity, we believe in and expect the fulfilment of His Plan ; the hallowing of the whole Universe, seen and unseen. He is there first, the Fountain of life and of generosity ; and therefore the travail of the worlds that lie upon His bosom, and are supported and penetrated by His Spirit, can have no meaning unless perfection is their term. It is true that in the course of this long history much will be discarded ; as much in our own lives is discarded—often at the cost of pain—as we move on. Much that we, with our short sight and feeble telescopes, take for destruction or ultimate loss, is a phase in His deep work of transmutation : a necessity, an austerity, of love. But beyond every apparent death is a life. I expect resurrection. " God is the Lord, through whom we escape death," says the Psalmist : we enter with our full surrender to His action another level of being, where our lives are fulfilled in His life.

" Whosoever shall leave all for my sake shall receive in this world a thousandfold, and in the world to come life everlasting." That is one of those promises of which all can see the fulfilment here and now. For what the human spirit desires above all in this world is to have its being justified, to be used, feel there is some meaning in that which it attempts and undergoes, some place for it in the mysterious process of life. And here those who relax their clutch on what we absurdly call " the " world, and give themselves to the real world of charity, redemptive action, co-operation with God, do receive a thousandfold. They receive an increasing and astonishing enrichment of existence, a deepening sense of significance in every joy, sacrifice, accomplishment and pain ; in fact, a genuine share in that creative life of God which is always coming, always entering, to refresh and enhance our life.

Through the Christian revelation men were shown, in a way that they could receive though never wholly understand, the nature of that Absolute Love which moves to their destiny all stars and all souls. And the term of that process is the Eternal Life, the perfect consummation which God has prepared for those that love Him ; in other words, all who really want it. " This is eternal life ; to know thee, the one true God "—have our eyes opened on the Fact of facts, the soul's unique satisfaction, Whom to know is to adore. Christ in His great intercession asked only this for those He loved ; this real life, poised in God. " That they may be in us " ; each tiny separate spirit absorbed in the mighty current of the Divine Charity. " I in them and thou in me, that they may be perfected into one " ; this is the consummation we look for, that share in the life of Reality which is prepared for men.

And further, the history of those souls whom that living God awakens, besets, and purifies by the action of His stern untiring love is unintelligible unless within that real life, all those faculties He is here bringing forth in them achieve the perfection which here they never reach. We are to expect the pure joy of a keen, unbaffled intelligence, of an unhindered vision of beauty ; ears that can hear what the universe is always trying to say to us, hearts at last capable of a pure and unlimited love. Then that sense of reaching forward, of coming up to the verge of a world of unbounded realities, which haunts our best moments of prayer and communion, will be fulfilled. " I look for the life of the world to come," and see hints of it everywhere.

And surely Christians, for whom the whole of life is ruled by a devoted faith in One God Whose nature is Charity ; One Lord, His eternal Thought, self-given in sacrifice ; one Spirit, who is the Giver of all life, have here a deep responsibility. Working for, trusting, expecting the complete manifestation of that Triune Love—that is, the redemption of the universe—must be the aim and motive of our inward and outward life. The Body of Christ exists to work for the world's transformation ; to bring Eternal Life into time, by the faithful and arduous incarnation of its faith and love in concrete acts. It is an organ of the Spirit, not a devotional guild. So its efforts cannot cease till its frontiers embrace the whole created order in its power, mystery and beauty : till the whole of life's energy is running right, sublimated, woven into that robe of many colours which clothes the Thought of God, and at the heart of the Universe, ruling it in its most majestic sweep and in its homeliest detail, we find His uttered Word and active Love.

This is the splendid vision on which our creed closes : and it means that all the marvellous and varied energies of physical and mental life, as well as those we attribute to spiritual life—all devoted service of beauty and truth, all heroic adventure, all the mysterious splendours of music and art—can become part of the Divine triumph and serve the Divine end. However adverse conditions may seem to be, Christians must never deflect from this aim through weariness, or religious self-indulgence; never doubt its ultimate achievement. The cynical or pessimistic attitude, silent acquiescence in second-rate standards of thought or action, selfish politics tending to war or hatred, incomes drawn from dubious industries, all public or private manifestations of pride, anger, envy, greed—these things are impossible for Christians ; they are betrayals of trust. In one or other of these departments every human life, however humble, can do something to hasten or retard the triumph of the Eternal Charity. For God is not the God of the invisible creation alone. The new, more real life that we expect must penetrate every level of existence, and every relationship—politics, industry, science, art, our attitude to each other, our attitude to living nature—spiritualizing and unselfing all this ; subduing it to the transforming action of " the intellectual radiance full of love."

This is the work which has been delegated to us, energetic spirits created in the image of the Absolute Charity, and placed within His half-made world to further His plan ; and we are required to begin now. Faith is not a refuge from reality. It is a demand that we face reality, with all its difficulties, opportunities and implications. The true subject-matter of religion is not our own little souls, but the Eternal God and His whole mysterious purpose, and our solemn responsibility to Him. " Ye are of God, little children ; greater is He that is in you than he that is in the world." It is within our power to bring in the Kingdom, if our courage and generosity are equal to our faith.

There it is, in its eternal power and beauty. Angels and Archangels, energies and worlds—the ever-widening universe which science discloses to us, and the more mysterious, more deeply sacred worlds which are glimpsed through the veils of beauty and holiness—all centred on the Word, the Thought of God, nourished and supported by His unmeasured Charity. And we, " being made children of God and of the Light," are committed to a steady, loyal effort in our own small place and way, to the ever more perfect incarnation of that Kingdom in space and time. Each Godward glance translated into sacrificial action, each deed inspired by generosity, each deliberate contradiction of self-interest and self-will, helps it on. In some way each of us must set our hands to this, if we desire to take up our birthright as children of God.

If we refuse—if we do not at least try to manifest something of the Creative Charity in our dealings with life, whether by action, thought or prayer, and do it at our own cost—if we roll up the talent of love in the nice white napkin of piety and put it safely out of the way, sorry that the world is so hungry and thirsty, so sick and so fettered, and leave it at that : then, even that little talent may be taken from us. We may discover at the crucial moment that we are spiritually bankrupt. From him that hath not shall be taken away even that which he hath. It is a critical moment now for the Church of Christ ; and that means for each Christian, since we are the Church. It is for us to show the puzzled and uneasy world the saving nature and practical import of that revelation of Reality made in Christ ; a revelation which only becomes convincing to others in the degree in which we suffer for it, take risks for it, give it priority over self-interest and self-will. This is our terrible privilege. If we do not exercise it, no one else can. "These know that thou didst send me." They know that the Divine Immanence is really the Divine Charity; and only by dwelling in Charity, unlimited generosity, can they dwell in Reality, in God. On us, then, lies the full responsibility of declaring this spiritual standard and working for this spiritual goal; "the life of the age that is drawing near."

This obligation is to be looked at in the most concrete and practical way. Large thoughts about world-movements usually bring the comforting conviction that we cannot do much about them ourselves. But the greatest of all world-movements began with a handful of devoted and confident souls, who risked all for their belief and their love; who knew they possessed something and therefore were willing to give it; who were looking all the time, with an absolute and trustful certitude, for more abundant life. The Creed, which is the rule of our prayer, requires of us this same attitude, because we too believe this about God.

If history is the dramatic expression of mankind's corporate thinking and striving, beyond and within all that corporate thinking and striving is the immense energy of man's corporate faith and prayer; the trustful stretching out towards an unseen Reality, the humble Godward life of countless souls. That inarticulate aspiration, that "blind intent" as the mystics say, always reaching out to the deep fountains of eternal peace, is a factor of which we seldom think enough. Yet here is man's deepest contact with that unmoved Truth in which the created order is immersed, and which is ever seeking fresh channels whereby to enter, cleanse and refresh the world. To become such a channel is the chief aim of the interior life. We shall only achieve it if a trustful adoration and a limitless self-offering govern our prayer, more and more laying open the very depths of our being here and now to the pressure of that Unchanging God, Who accomplishes His creative work by means of those very creatures He has made.

It is in the midst of time, with the clock ticking, the engagement-book bristling, the tube running a two-minute service, and every new edition of the paper recording some new movement, new sin, new sorrow of the restless world, that we have to find and live that eternal life, which consists in the disclosure of the Divine Charity. We are to bring forth the " fruits of the Spirit " here and now, enmeshed as we are in the complex anxieties of our material and emotional life ; ever holding tight to the deep tranquillity of that Unchanging God who comes to us in the "sacrament of the present moment," and meeting and receiving Him there with gratitude, however baffling the outward form of that sacrament may be. Our whole life is to be poised on a certain glad expectancy of God ; taking each moment, incident, choice and opportunity as material placed in our hand by the Creator whose whole intricate and mysterious process moves towards the triumph of Charity, and who has given each living spirit a tiny part in this vast work of transformation.

It is a real part, even though its precise character and importance may not be clear to us ; though we may not perhaps see much result from it during our own short span, or have any clear view of the strange design from which the hidden Artist is working. We should elude much enfeebling spiritual worry, and proportionately increase our effective contribution to the world's redemption if we kept more steadily in mind the patent fact of our own

limited knowledge : that the richness and splendour of
the spiritual universe which surrounds and penetrates our
narrow universe of sense is mostly unperceived by us as
we are now. It is true that as spirits, anchored to this
world yet belonging to that, we do already live within
that spiritual universe. But like new-born kittens, our
eyes are not yet opened to our situation ; we can only
vaguely recognize the touch upon the fur.

The narrow limits within which even the physical
world is accessible to us, might warn us of the folly of
drawing negative conclusions about the world that is not
seen. We cannot penetrate far into the reality of any life
other than our own. The plants and the animals keep
their own strange secret; and it is already a sign of maturity
when we recognize that they have a secret to keep, that
their sudden disclosures of beauty, their power of awaken-
ing tenderness and delight, warn us that here too we are
in the presence of children of the One God. With what
a shock of surprise, either enchantment or horror, we meet
the impact of any truly new experience ; its abrupt re-
minder that we do really live among worlds unrealized.
Our limited spectrum of colour, with its hints of a more
delicate loveliness beyond our span, our narrow scale of
sound : these, we know, are mere chunks cut out of a
world of infinite colour and sound—the world that is drawing near, charged with the unbearable splendour and music
of the Absolute God. And beyond this, as our spiritual
sensibility develops, sparkles and brief intoxications of
pure beauty, and messages from the heart of an Unfathomable Life come now and then to delight us : hints of an
aspect of His Being which the careful piety that dare not
look over the hedge of the paddock will never find. All
this, then, should warn us that humility and common

sense both require an attitude of loving ignorance, of trustful acceptance, as regards that supernatural life which is always pressing in on us, always waiting for us; as truly there as the cosmic life of infinite space and duration into which we are suddenly caught, when we look for the first time through a great telescope at the awful galaxy of the stars.

The stay-at-home Englishman, going for the first time to great mountains, cannot know or guess the true quality of the experience which lies before him. All the guide books and photographs—even the strange exciting literature of Alpine adventure—tell him little or nothing of that enlarging, humbling, cleansing and exalting revelation, which comes from fresh and personal contact with a wholly new aspect of our world. There it is, in its majesty and aloofness : waiting for him, living its own life, but only to be apprehended by those who make the venture of faith. So too the Mystery of God remains a mystery. We believe in, we cannot yet conceive in its independent splendour and reality, that world which in moments of communion we feel to be very near. The life which is ruled by its own deep longing for God, and is really moving in the direction of God, is always moving towards that Country. But it is not easy to realize that, while the train with its unexhilarating apparatus of sleeping berths and restaurant cars runs through long tunnels and cuttings, and over interminable stretches of agricultural land.

When the traveller enters Switzerland, and draws up the blind—perhaps somewhere near Berne—in the early morning, he may see on the far horizon a line of snow. To his tired eyes it does not look very much : a sign perhaps, but a sign that is very far away. Yet somehow, that white line calms, refreshes and exhilarates, for it proves that he is getting there ; that he is, after all, living in a world which is not all tenement dwellings, factories and potato fields, not entirely subdued to the requirements of the pumping station and electric grid. The majesty of the eternal snow is really there. He glimpses the substance of things hoped for, the evidence of things not seen. What we call " religious experience " is rather like the pulling up of that blind. As the train rushes on, or lingers in sordid stations covered with advertisements and entirely destitute of any view, that glimpse reminds us of the solitude and awful beauty of the spiritual summits; the demand on the utmost endurance of those who are called to them, the long and steady climb, the risks, the hardships, and the unspeakable reward.

It is true that we cannot conceive all that it means and all that it costs to stand in that world of purity and wonder from which the saints speak to us ; those high solitudes where they taste the mountain rapture, the deeply hidden valleys with a vista of white splendour at the end, the torrents of living water, the quiet upper pastures, and the tiny holy flowers. But because we believe in One God, the Eternal Perfect, His love and faithfulness and beauty, so we believe in that world prepared for all who love Him; where He shall be All, in all.